A Dog's Best Friend

A DOG'S BEST FRIEND

*The secrets that make good
dog owners great*

JAN FENNELL

ISIS
LARGE PRINT
Oxford

First published in Great Britain 2004
by
HarperCollins*Publishers*

Published in Large Print 2005 by ISIS Publishing Ltd,
7 Centremead, Osney Mead, Oxford OX2 0ES
by arrangement with
HarperCollins*Publishers*

British Library Cataloguing in Publication Data
Fennell, Jan
    A dog's best friend.– Large print ed.
    1. Dogs – Training
    2. Dogs – Psychology
    3. Human-animal relationships
    4. Large type books
    I. Title
    636.7'0887

ISBN 0–7531–5649–0 (hb)
ISBN 0–7531–5650–4 (pb)

Printed and bound by Antony Rowe, Chippenham

For my grandchildren
Ceri-Ann, Bethan and Ben

Contents

INTRODUCTION

When my book *The Dog Listener* was first published, I had no idea it would connect with such a wide audience. It is a source of constant pride to me that so many people have turned to the compassionate communication method advocated in its pages. By rejecting the aggressive and damaging ideas of the past, they have displayed the open-mindedness and, I like to think, intelligence that instantly separates the good owner from the bad one. They have made an important first step.

Perhaps the greatest lesson I have learned since the publication of that book (and its sequel, *The Practical Dog Listener*) is that people's desire to improve the quality of the life they share with their dogs is limitless. The world, it seems, is full of owners dedicated to becoming the companions their dogs really deserve. I am always meeting people eager to deepen their knowledge still further, to develop into not just good owners but great ones.

But what is it that makes a great owner? What are the qualities that distinguish these people from the rest? These are questions that I'm asked all the time and, if I'm honest, have often struggled to answer — to my own satisfaction at least.

I have met all kinds of owners in the course of my life and career. A few have been awful, unfit even to own a dog in my opinion, but most have been good, caring people, genuinely interested in making their dog's life a happy one. Along the way, it has been my good fortune to have met people whose characters and abilities have elevated them above the rest, owners who have made a lasting impact on me, and about whom I'd use the word "great" without hesitation.

It was while thinking about some of these people recently that the idea for this book was born. I had been asked for the umpteenth time what it is that makes a great owner, what separates them from the rest, when suddenly it occurred to me that if there *is* a simple answer to that question, then these exceptional people would be able to provide it. It struck me that if I shared their stories, explaining what they taught me and, in so doing, highlighting their strengths and qualities, then I might go a long way towards defining the kind of outstanding ownership to which so many people aspire.

It wasn't long before I was drawing together memories of individuals who have impressed me, not only as owners and people but also as independent thinkers. As I moved on to analyse what it was each of them gave me, so this book took shape.

The owners who feature in these pages are a diverse bunch. Some are family members who sowed important seeds in my younger life, others are people who played a pivotal role in leading me to develop my method. Some have inspired me by example, others have helped me develop my methods or sharpen my thinking since I took my work out into the wider world.

One or two have simply made me appreciate just how deep the well of human kindness runs when it comes to dogs.

Yet, for all their differences, they share one thing in common. Each of them has — or had — a special bond with man's best friend. And each passed on to me something valuable about the way we live with dogs. By absorbing their lessons, I hope everyone can take that next step and become not just a good owner, but a great one.

Jan Fennell
North Lincolnshire, Spring 2004

"HOW WOULD YOU FEEL?"

Why great owners put themselves in their dog's place

Our attitude to dogs — and to the animal world in general — has gone through enormous changes in my lifetime. During my childhood in post-war London, most people would have treated the modern notion of animal rights and welfare with disdain. It would have brought me little but ridicule to espouse in public the sort of compassionate training ideas I do now.

Yet, even fifty or so years ago, these seemingly modern ideas were already alive and blossoming in places. I was lucky enough to grow up within a family who viewed our relationship with animals — and dogs in particular — in a way that was unusual for the time. Ours was a family of horse and dog lovers, and no one had a deeper affinity for both than my great-uncle Jim.

Uncle Jim was in his eighties when I was a little girl but was still a remarkable character. His colourful life included a spell with Buffalo Bill Cody's world-famous Wild West Show, an experience that had provided him with an unusual attitude to animals. I remember him telling me about the time he spent with the troupe's Native Americans. Their empathy with the show's horses had a deep impact on him, so much so that he had an almost telepathic relationship with Kitty, the lovely little black pony which pulled his vegetable cart around the streets of Fulham, Hammersmith and West London in the 1950s.

Some of my earliest and warmest childhood memories are of Uncle Jim, laying down the reins, putting his arms around me and gently whispering, "Take us home, Kit." Sure enough, Kitty would pick her way through the streets, like a homing pigeon.

Looking back on it now, it was Uncle Jim and Kitty who first instilled in me the idea of animals and humans working together in harmony. Uncle Jim used to talk about the way his Native American colleagues told him to "breathe with the horse". He and Kitty worked instinctively as a team. There was no coercion — they understood each other perfectly — and, as a result, their partnership seemed like the most natural thing in the world.

As a little girl I used to spend long hours sitting on the pony and trap with Uncle Jim. I saw many things that captured my imagination, but nothing quite so thought-provoking as what I witnessed outside, of all places, a pub one lunchtime.

Uncle Jim and his fellow street vendors lent real character to their area of London. They were a colourful collection of individuals, each on their pony and trap, clattering through the streets, living by a code that went back to an earlier age. One of their traditions was to meet up at various watering holes. It wasn't hard to spot where they were gathered — neatly arranged ranks of horses and carts would form outside.

Jim and his friends would put nosebags and blankets on their horses, then pop inside for a couple of hard-earned pints. If I was with Jim, he'd always get me a glass of lemonade and a packet of crisps to eat out on the cart. I was quite happy there, particularly when a friend of Jim — a rag-and-bone man called Albie — left me in the company of his dog Danny.

Albie was famous for travelling everywhere with Danny. As most dogs were at that time, Danny was a crossbreed, or "multi-pedigree" as I like to call them now. He would sit upright at Albie's side, as if he was his eyes and ears, which given his master's advancing years, sometimes he probably was.

One lunchtime, Albie and Jim arrived at the pub and were tending to their horses. Danny, as usual, had been put up on the trap with me.

Albie was very affectionate towards Danny, unusually so for the time. "You stay there now, there's a good boy," he told his dog, ruffling his neck as he placed him on the seat next to me.

As Albie was doing this, another rag-and-bone man had pulled up alongside.

He had seen Albie talking to his dog like this and was shaking his head, as if in disbelief.

"What the hell are you talking to the mutt for?" he said, barely able to suppress a laugh. "You don't ask a dog to do something. You tell him."

Albie didn't take too kindly to this.

"Is that right?" he said. "So how do you expect good manners if you don't show good manners?"

The other man looked nonplussed.

"What are you on about?" he said.

Albie indicated to me. "If I wanted young Janice here to do something, what do you think would be the best way to get her to do it? Ask her nicely or show her the back of my hand?"

The other man simply shook his head, as if to say Albie was soft in the head. They soon disappeared into the pub, where — presumably — the argument carried on.

On the surface this may seem a small moment, nothing much to write home about. But to me, at the age of five or six, it struck a powerful chord.

The London of those days was a difficult place to make a living. We were still getting over the effects of the Second World War — my mother and father had found it particularly hard to readjust to life after their wartime experiences. And life was generally hard at that time, so the notion that dogs were deserving of anyone's time and effort was highly unusual. "It's just a dog," was a commonplace expression. Yet here was someone defending a dog as if it were a person. It was something I had never heard before, but I soon discovered it wasn't a unique view.

Another influential person in my childhood was my cousin Doreen. While I was younger, Doreen lived near us in West London with her family, but when I was ten or so, she moved to Welwyn Garden City, the utopian new community in Hertfordshire. We regularly visited them there, on Sundays, Bank Holidays and Christmas.

The move to the greener climes of Hertfordshire had an immediate impact on the family's lifestyle. It wasn't long before I discovered they had acquired a dog — a lovely, black and tan crossbreed puppy they named Tinker. Tinker belonged to the whole family, but early on it was clear that Doreen regarded him very much as her dog. Most of the time it was she who fed him and walked him. And she spent the most time playing with him.

He was not the first dog in the family — that was Bruce, a lovely white German shepherd one of my uncles had got from Battersea Dogs' Home. The mistreatment he suffered still haunts me to this day. I will never forget the way my uncle would tease him by placing a bar of chocolate high on a table, leaving Bruce to salivate as he looked at it. From the outset, however, it was clear that Doreen had a very different attitude to dogs.

Their house was always full of people. The first time I went there my cousin Paul was playing with a friend. I remember they were in the garden throwing a ball around. As part of their entertainment they put the ball in front of Tinker's face, then pulled it away again as he snapped to grab it. Paul had only done this a couple of times when Doreen appeared in the kitchen doorway. By coincidence, she happened to have a rolling pin in her hand. It made the sight of her all the more intimidating.

"You can stop that right away, young man. I won't have that," she said. "How would you like it if someone did that to you?"

The boy looked stunned, as I must have done. I had never heard anyone in the family defend a dog in that way before. But it wasn't long before I heard it again.

A little later that same day, Doreen's husband, Reg, appeared in the garden with a biscuit. Reg was fond of Tinker and would take him for walks, and the dog soon appeared at his side. "What's the matter? Want a bit of this do you?" he said playfully waving the biscuit around.

Doreen soon reappeared — this time without the rolling pin. He may have been the "man of the house", but the same rules applied.

"Reg, I won't have you teasing him like that. It might be fun for you, but it's not fun for the dog. How'd you like it?"

We all laughed, but I looked at Doreen's face and saw she was utterly serious. From then on, I became fascinated by her relationship with her dog.

Doreen was a wonderful person and I always looked forward to seeing her, but the fact she had such a lovely dog made each visit even more special. Doreen was very strict about what we could and couldn't do with her dog. Playing the retrieval games which Tinker enjoyed was fine. Taking him out for a walk without an adult, on the other hand, was not. "You're not responsible enough to take a dog out," she said, which again was something new and radical for me. Back in the streets of West London, children routinely walked dogs.

Doreen was absolutely consistent in her approach, no matter who was involved. On one occasion, I remember my father and his brother, Doreen's father, Fred, playing "piggy in the middle" with a ball and Tinker as the increasingly agitated "piggy". Doreen was upstairs, but the moment Tinker let out a distressed bark, she was bounding down the stairs.

"What do you think you're doing?" she asked them — it didn't matter that it was her father and uncle involved, two of the senior figures in the family.

My Dad put an arm around her and asked her to lighten up a little.

"Come on, Doreen, you think more of that dog than you do of us," he said.

But she was adamant. "He's my dog and I'm going to treat him my way and I'm not having it, Uncle Wal." And that was that.

On another occasion, her daughter Diane was trying to put a doll's bonnet on Tinker. Again there was no argument.

"Stop that, you have dolls for that," Doreen insisted. "The dog is not there for your entertainment."

Looking back, I can see that Doreen's approach worked. As Tinker grew up, I couldn't help noticing how much calmer he was than all the other dogs I'd come across. There was no rushing around, no barking and jumping up. I remember asking her one day, "How come Tinker's so happy, Doreen?"

"Because I haven't made him mixed up like so many other people do," she said. "Other people's dogs are so anxious all the time. No wonder, given the way people tease them and treat them badly. All I do is give some consideration to how he's feeling."

It was an attitude that was an extension of Doreen herself. She was the warmest, kindest person in my family. She was also someone who committed herself one hundred per cent to anything she did. To everybody else, "a dog was just a dog". But to Doreen it was a living creature, with feelings, with a soul.

As Tinker's training developed, so too did Doreen's ideas. She used food rewards in a way I'd never seen anyone do before. For instance: "Tinker's not going to do the right thing for nothing," she'd say. "He's not stupid."

My Uncle Fred would often see this and tell her she was spoiling him and turning him into a softie. "The dog should do it because you say so," he'd say.

She'd shoot him a look and reply: "You wouldn't."

As a young girl, sitting there on the fringes of all this, I remember thinking what common sense it sounded. But it was a long time before I understood what Albie and Doreen had instinctively sensed: that a dog was going to respond better if it was shown some respect and consideration, that you were going to have a better relationship by empathising with it, by trying to understand how it might feel to be in its position. It was a lesson worth waiting to learn.

THE TIES THAT BIND

Why great owners understand man's special relationship with dogs

Like everything else nowadays, people have a tendency to overcomplicate their relationship with their dogs. Too often, I think, we forget that ours is a simple partnership that dates back tens of thousands of years, to the time when our ancestors first domesticated the wolf, *Canis lupus*, to create the dog, *Canis familiaris*. Back then, man and dog were bound by a deep and instinctive understanding of each other's needs and nature. Man provided security, sanctuary, food and warmth; the dog provided its superior senses and hunting abilities. They shared a form of language and understood each other perfectly. They were a team, working intuitively together — and very successfully.

During the course of the millennia since then, man and dog have drifted apart. In the main, we have become strangers — rather than the best friends we like to call ourselves.

It has only been in recent years that I have begun to understand man's special relationship with the dog, to unravel fully the nature of the language the two species

once shared instinctively. That such special relationships existed, however, was something I'd learnt to
appreciate a lot earlier.

Two chance meetings during my childhood loom
large in the memory in this respect. The owners were
very different, but both sowed significant seeds.

Sometimes the most influential encounters are also the
briefest. So it proved during a summer's camping
holiday in Exmoor and Lorna Doone country back in
the 1960s. I was with my parents and the first dog I'd
ever been able to call my own, Shane — a beautiful
tricoloured collie my father had bought at a kennels
near Heathrow.

My father loved discovering country pubs and one
lunchtime went to a beautiful one near the village of
Oar — a picturesque spot, with views over the moor. It
was a gorgeous day and we sat outside on benches.
Shane found himself a comfortable spot under a tree,
where he was soon quietly snoozing.

The pub was a magnet for locals and tourists alike.
The local sheep market had been on that morning, so
that afternoon the place was crammed with farmers
and shepherds. Their Land Rovers and trailers filled the
car park. It was a very friendly place. People would say
hello as they went in and one or two of the farmers
stopped to admire Shane. "That's a lovely dog," one of
them said, giving Shane's neck a friendly ruffle.

Most of the farmers arrived alone, but one turned up
with a lovely looking Border collie. I don't remember

the farmer's name, but I do recall the dog's — she was called Tina.

There was something about their relationship that struck me straight away. Tina looked at her owner with a focus and intensity that seemed unusual. I remember noticing that he barely needed to give her an instruction before she did exactly what he wanted. As he headed into the pub, for instance, he just said "stay" and she was down on all fours, sitting passively on the grass.

The pair seemed to have a great understanding of each other. When he emerged again, he had a pint of beer and a clean ashtray, which he placed on the grass next to Tina. He then poured a small splash of beer into the tray. Tina was soon slurping happily away. What a perfect pair they made, I thought to myself.

With people arriving all the time, the tables were filling up fast. Soon the table next to ours was taken by a group of half a dozen or so farmers, including Tina's owner. The air was soon heavy with farming talk — everything from lamb prices at that morning's market to the quality of that year's crops and the weather. They were soon engaging us in conversation as well.

"So where did you get this handsome boy?" one of them asked me.

I explained that we had got him from a kennels in West London.

The farmer told me he too had a Border collie.

"So where's he today then?" I asked, surprised at his absence.

"Oh, he's a working dog. He stays on the farm where he belongs," he replied.

Tina's owner was sitting opposite this man. I looked at him and said: "You've got your dog with you. You don't agree, do you?"

"No, I don't, young lady," he said with a wink.

His friends were soon rolling their eyes heavenward. "Oh, here we go," said one.

Almost immediately, the other five farmers were taking it in turns to explain their difference of opinion over Tina. Each of them had collies, but each of them had left them back in their kennels on their respective farms. They simply didn't believe that a working dog should be included in a farmer's social life.

"He's made that dog too soft," one said, pointing at Tina.

"She even goes in the house with him," said another.

Tina's owner didn't seem perturbed by this. He'd clearly heard it all before. But when everyone had had their say, he turned to me and explained his side of the argument.

"The way I see it, Tina works hard for me every day. She does everything I ask of her and there's nothing wrong with her switching off and enjoying herself with me every now and again," he said.

As the sun shone and the beer flowed, the conversation continued. It wasn't aggressive — there were lots of smiles and winks — but there was no doubting that everyone was absolutely serious about their positions within the argument. It was one of those situations where no one was going to give ground.

12

Tina's owner was quite calm and relaxed about it all. The other five farmers were more agitated, but they weren't yielding an inch, either. Everyone agreed to disagree.

At one point, as the argument continued, someone mentioned the fact that Tina competed very successfully in the local sheepdog trials. When I asked the other farmers whether their dogs competed, they all answered "yes". "Tina's got a knack for it though, and she usually wins," one of them grudgingly admitted.

"So what about your dog then, young lady?" one of the farmers asked, trying to deflect the subject for a while. "Do you work him at all?"

"Oh no, he's a pet," I said.

"I hope you don't mind me saying, but I don't think collies should be pets," one of the farmers said. "Their instinct is to herd and work, not sit around in a house all day."

Until now my father had sat there, quietly chatting to my mother, but this comment clearly annoyed him and he couldn't let it pass. By now both Shane and Tina were sprawled out under the shade of the trees, relishing the afternoon sun and oblivious to the fuss. My father pointed at them and said, "Look at those two. Does either of them look like they're being mistreated?"

Although it was a good line and got a good laugh, it brought the conversation to a close. The farmers had soon set off on their way back to their farms, but the memory of that argument lingered for a long time afterwards.

I had admired the way the farmer had stuck to his guns. He had been doing what he felt was right and no amount of criticism or ribbing from his colleagues was going to change that opinion. But what stuck in my mind more, was the natural way he and Tina had had with each other. When I saw people out walking their pets, struggling to get along, I would wonder why it was that the farmer and his dog had such a perfect partnership in comparison.

Now, of course, I can see that theirs was a relationship deep-rooted in shared instincts and mutual understanding that dates back millennia. They represented a tradition and dependency that barely survives. I now understand that it was no coincidence that Tina's owner was more successful in sheepdog trials than the other shepherds. The bond between the two was so strong, they must have been a formidable pair to watch at work.

Evidence of this natural, intuitive bond between man and dog was thin on the ground in the London of my youth. People tended to take their dogs for granted. They got on with their lives and the dogs got on with theirs. On the street where I lived, several dogs were allowed to roam freely. Provided they didn't misbehave, life went on. If they did step out of line, the punishment meted out could be harsh.

In the wake of my encounter with the farmer, I occasionally came across owners with similarly unusual attitudes. It was one such person who provided me with another insight to store away for later in my life.

★ ★ ★

One morning I was walking Shane in a local park with my father. At the far corner of the park, we saw a collection of lorries and caravans. It was early autumn and the first fair of the season had arrived in our neck of the woods.

As we got closer to the mini-village that had sprung up there, we were suddenly aware of a rather large, black German shepherd. In those days — as now — German shepherds had an undeserved reputation for being aggressive and occasionally violent. As this one came out and looked at us, my father instinctively drew Shane back and put him back on the lead. But it was soon obvious he had no cause for concern. It was as if there was an invisible barrier there — the German shepherd took two steps towards us then stopped. I was confused as to why it had done this, but soon it was clear it had responded to its owner, a rather scruffy looking figure who was soon walking towards us.

"Morning, lovely day, isn't it?" he said.

"Morning, yes, smashing," my father replied. "I was just looking at your dog. Have you got him on an invisible line or something?" he joked. "I've never seen one of them so well behaved."

The man turned round to look at his dog, still standing perfectly still.

"Oh, he just knows his boundaries — all my dogs do," he smiled.

My father had a keen interest in dogs too and got chatting to the man. It turned out he had half a dozen or so dogs, mainly for guarding the valuables that he and his family took with them as they travelled the country with the fair.

He talked about how he trained them, then got each of them to specialise in different tasks around the fair. "You want them to frighten the right people," he said, at one point, gesturing to me. "They're no use to me if they scare little girls away from my rides."

It was clear that this was someone who knew a lot about dogs. "Do you mind if I ask you a question?" I said nervously.

"Not at all, young lady, fire away," he said, smiling.

In recent weeks, one problem had been obsessing me above all others. It had all begun with a prank played by a kid called Ronnie in Rowallan Road in Fulham, where I lived at the time.

The most popular toy of the day was a thing called a "cracker" — a triangular piece of cardboard with a piece of paper folded inside it. It looked innocuous enough, but when you flicked this thing it made a really sharp cracking noise.

I was walking down Rowallan Road with Shane one day when Ronnie jumped out and let out this huge crack. It made me jump, but it sent Shane into the most terrible spin. It was the beginning of a nervous streak that had grown progressively worse. It was now so bad that he even became agitated at the sound of rain rapping on the windows outside. Bonfire night was still some way off, but it had already become a date to dread as far as I was concerned.

I had tried all sorts of things, but mainly reassuring Shane with a cuddle. It had somehow made matters worse rather than better. Here was someone who clearly understood dogs more deeply than I did. What was there to lose in asking?

"How do the dogs cope with the noise? What with all the squeals and whoops coming from the rides, it must be frightening for them?"

"No, love, none of my dogs are afraid of noises," he said. "I just leave them to it."

"What do you mean?" I said, a bit confused.

"Well, there's nothing to fear, is there? We all know that. So if we behave as if there's nothing to fear, they'll get the message eventually."

I thought perhaps he had a point, so I decided I'd try his advice out the next time it rained. I didn't have to wait long. A few nights later, there was a particularly heavy downpour. Shane went into a funk as usual — but this time I tried to resist the urge to cuddle him. I carried on reading and playing records in my room as if nothing was happening, trying desperately to relay the message that there was nothing to fear.

At the age of fifteen, you expect everything to happen in an instant. As far as I could see my behaviour was having next to no effect on Shane, who was now cowering under my bed. I loved Shane so much, I couldn't bear the sight of him distressed. Soon he was cuddled up alongside me on top of the bed, shivering as the winds drove the rain against the window pane with even greater intensity.

Hindsight is, of course, a marvellous thing. Now I know I was doing the complete opposite of what I should have been doing. More than anything else

17

Shane needed to be assured there was nothing wrong. And he needed to be assured by a figure in whom he had absolute trust and confidence. Instead, I had made two cardinal errors. First, I had been inconsistent, changing my mind about how to deal with the situation and giving poor Shane mixed signals in the process. Then, when I came to cuddle him, I had confirmed his worst fears — the rain was something to feel threatened by and to hide from after all. My intentions had been good, but in the end I had only added to his anxiety.

Eventually I would see the wisdom of the words of the man from the fair. The ideas he implanted in my mind would grow into one of the fundamental building blocks of my method. But if only I'd been old — and wise — enough to have understood them at the time, Shane's life might have been a slightly happier one.

"WHAT'S IN IT FOR ME?"

Why great owners work with, not against, their dogs

Dogs operate according to a simple rule — the "What's in It for Me?" principle. In essence, any owner wanting to get willing cooperation from their dog has to work on the understanding that it — like them — works according to fundamentally selfish instincts. It is not going to do something unless there is a tangible benefit from doing so. This was something I first glimpsed with my cousin Doreen and her attitude to Tinker. But it was another forward-thinking member of the family who taught me how productive this idea could really be.

My Uncle George was the oldest of my father's five siblings and he lived with my Aunt Ellen at their home in West London, near Heathrow Airport. We visited them often and I always looked forward to the trip, again mainly because it meant I could spend time with a dog — in this case their black and tan crossbreed, Rex.

Rex was a mixture of all sorts of breeds — he probably had some German shepherd in him

19

somewhere — and had a curly tail, big pointy ears and a slightly foxy look. He was a hugely affectionate dog and always made a beeline for me when I visited George and Ellen. While the rest of the family chatted away, I'd sit out in the garden, stroking him or playing ball.

George was in his late fifties by then, retired from his job as a lorry driver. He was a straightforward, down-to-earth man and his relationship with his dog was absolutely typical of the period. They were very relaxed with each other. Rex would sit by Uncle George's feet most of the time and would go out with him every morning to get the newspaper. There were no big shows of affection or emotion, but that was the way in those days. As for training, I don't think the idea had ever occurred to him.

Rex was a happy dog and I have no doubt George cared for him deeply too, but he did have one habit that drove George round the bend. On a regular basis, he would go into the garden and begin digging ferociously around the large flower beds, and the roses in particular. George wasn't best pleased with this, to say the least. He and Ellen were very proud of their garden, and spent long hours tending it. Their lawn was immaculate, as smooth as a billiard table, but their roses were their pride and joy.

They were not a generation to analyse things in depth, so there was little discussion about the reason for Rex's behaviour. Whether he was marking territory or simply digging for a hidden bone, they were not interested. All that concerned them was how this was going to be stopped.

George had tried all sorts of things. He had shouted at the dog, and at one point thrown his slipper at him out of frustration. On one occasion, he confessed, he had given Rex "a good kick up the backside". But nothing had worked. People had made all sorts of suggestions and my dad had suggested he build a fence around the rose beds, but George had rejected that.

Ellen, to her credit, tried to defuse the situation. At times, there was an echo of my cousin Doreen's caring philosophy in her comments. "Don't blame the dog," she said on one occasion. "It's only in our eyes that he's doing bad. He doesn't know any different."

This did little to ease George's frustration — all he could do was curse Rex every time he attacked his roses.

Then, one summer, the solution presented itself in the most unlikely form of Freddie, one of George's nephews (and my cousins). Freddie was three and the son of George's and my father's sister, Mary Ann (known to everyone as Sis). Just as no one referred to Sis by her real name, so we all called Freddie by his nickname — Sticky Fingers. Sis was very relaxed in her parenting and she allowed Freddie to eat as many sweets as he liked. As a result, he constantly had his hands in the sweet jars that sat on everyone's sideboards in those days. What was really unpleasant was the way he would remove half-eaten sweets or bits of chocolate from his mouth and save them for later. By the time he had left someone's house after a visit, there were bits of sweet or chocolate stuck to the floor, carpet, furniture — everywhere. It was a particularly unpleasant habit.

He was only three, but I can remember the family having a mini council of war about his behaviour. My mother was very house-proud and wouldn't have him anywhere near her home. And, slowly but surely, other family members were conveniently forgetting to invite Sis and Fred to family events too.

"It's not nice for Sis. We should tell her," someone said.

"But who? I don't fancy it," someone else responded.

It was my father who emerged as the unlikely saviour of the day. One weekend, quite out of the blue, Sis, Fred and Freddie turned up on the doorstep of our home in Fulham. I could almost feel my mother's blood pressure rising as they made their way into her immaculate living room. Immediately, Freddie spotted our sweet jar and dived in, as was his wont. My father could see my mother panicking and wove her away to make a cup of tea. "I'll keep an eye on Freddie, love," he said reassuringly.

Sure enough, within a minute or two Freddie had removed a half-eaten sweet from his mouth. He was about to leave it on a chair when my father moved into action. As Freddie searched for the right spot to deposit the sticky toffee, my father took it off him and promptly deposited it in a nearby bin.

He chose his words carefully. "If you take it out of your mouth, Freddie, it goes in the bin and you can't

22

have it back," he said with a smile. He didn't want to chastise him — just get his message across.

Predictably, it didn't sink in immediately. At the sight of his sweet being thrown away, Freddie burst out crying and ran off to Sis. When my father explained what had happened, she looked a little embarrassed and had no option but to accept what he said. "Be a good boy, Freddie, and listen to your Uncle Wal," she said.

It wasn't long before Freddie was back in the sweet jar. Soon, he was once more reaching to take the sweet out of his mouth. And once more my father moved towards him with his arm outstretched. "Is that one going in the bin too, Freddie?" he asked.

"No," Freddie replied before popping the sweet back in his mouth.

It carried on like this for the hour or so Sis and Fred remained with us, my father spending every minute watching Freddie like a hawk. Each time he went to take a sweet from his mouth my father intercepted him. By the time they were ready to leave the penny had dropped. Freddie was still eating sweets — but he was finishing each one before going on to the next.

My father thought this was a real triumph. When we next went over to George and Ellen's a week or so later, he took great pride in proclaiming he had "cured Freddie", then telling the story in great detail.

"He got the message soon enough," he said. "He saw what would happen if he did the wrong thing."

Everyone in the family thought it was the funniest thing ever.

"Why did nobody think of doing that before?" my Aunt Ellen giggled. "It's so obvious."

The only one who wasn't laughing was Uncle George, whom I remember vividly sitting nodding away to himself.

"You've given me an idea there, Wal," he said after a while. "I might try that with Rex."

I don't think anyone was quite sure what he meant. But it became clear when we next went back to their house. This time it was George who was wearing the triumphant expression.

"I've sorted out Rex's habit of digging up the rose bed," he told my father, before going on to explain what had been going on since our last visit.

My father's success with Sticky Fingers Freddie had lit a light bulb in George's head. He decided that Rex needed to learn a similar lesson — and immediately set about providing it.

George had been sitting in the garden one evening that week when he'd seen Rex digging away in the rose bed once more. Immediately he'd walked over to him, grabbed him by the collar and marched him unceremoniously into the house, where he'd deposited him in the utility room.

"I left him in there to have a think about it for half an hour or so," he said.

Rex had whined a little, but George had ignored it.

When George opened the utility room door, he found Rex lying there with a sheepish look on his face. Released back into the garden again, he wandered around aimlessly for a while, shooting George the odd glance. A few minutes later, George popped back into the kitchen to talk to Ellen. When he returned he found Rex scratching away in the flower beds again. Without saying a word, he marched over, took Rex by the collar and repeated the operation, this time leaving the dog in the utility room for a few minutes more.

"I didn't raise my voice to him or get rough at all. I just did it."

That had been a couple of weeks ago. Today, as we sat in the garden, Rex was playing with me and the other children as usual. At one stage, the ball he was retrieving ran into the rose beds. He was about to set foot on the soil when he saw George make a move as if to get up. He moved away immediately.

George was clearly feeling chuffed with himself. But then, late in the afternoon, he noticed Rex digging away again — only this time in the compost heap at the far end of the garden. He got up out of his chair but got no reaction. "What am I going to do now?" he asked Ellen.

"Well, he's obviously learned something and I'd rather he dug there than in the rose bed," she said. "Leave him for now."

This seemed to please George. George admitted to my father that he didn't enjoy meting out physical punishment. "I didn't like hurting him," he said. As the afternoon wore on Rex came over to lie at George's feet as usual. "We understand each other now, don't we, mate," he said ruffling his coat.

George and Rex went on to live a long and happy life together. They were close anyway, but afterwards they seemed even greater pals, happier than ever in each other's company.

People are not born good dog owners; they need to learn to adapt, to show some thought. Sometimes they also need to admit when they've gone wrong. To my mind, what was remarkable about Uncle George was that he admitted he was failing with Rex. Rather than taking it out on the dog, as so many owners of that generation would have done, he applied his mind and came up with another approach.

Like my father, he was an uneducated man. He had left school at twelve, forced by the economic realities of the time to earn a living to help his family. Yet he'd been smart enough to work this situation out and come up with a successful non-violent solution.

It was a long time before I fully understood what he'd tapped into. Eventually I came to see that he had been using positive association to get the message across to Rex. But it was only when I fully understood the true, underlying nature of that positive association that the power of that method really struck me.

Now I understand that as pack-dwelling animals, dogs instinctively see safety in numbers, that they like to work as a member of a team. To be excluded from a pack, as Rex was, is the ultimate punishment to most dogs. In the wild, it can effectively be a death sentence. So to threaten a dog with banishment from a pack, as George had done, is a tool that can produce quite remarkable results.

It was among the most important lessons I have ever been given. And for that, I will always be grateful to dear old Uncle George.

OUR MUTUAL FRIENDS

Why respect is the key to a great relationship with dogs

As most of us know from personal experience, no relationship is ever simple or straightforward. Life, with all its uncertainties, has an unpleasant habit of making sure that difficult times are never far away. For this reason, every relationship needs a few fundamental qualities if it is going to survive all that life has to throw at it.

It was a man called Jim Moss who made me see that this applies as much to our relationship with our dogs as it does to those with our fellow humans. Thirty years ago, in his own quiet way, Jim taught me that the key to any successful relationship can be summed up in one simple word: respect.

Jim and his wife Amy were the most devoted couple you could ever have hoped to meet. I met them in the 1970s, when, with my then husband and two young children, I left London for the Lincolnshire village of Firsby. It was a small, tight-knit community and Jim and Amy were among its most popular figures. A retired couple, both were keen gardeners and walkers, but their greatest passion in life was each other.

You never saw Jim without Amy, or vice versa. They went everywhere together, did everything together. They were also the most polite, kind-hearted people — salt-of-the-earth sorts who'd do anything to help. Everyone thought the world of them.

Occasionally, I would drop in to see them and have a cup of tea. I remember once the conversation got around to marriage — and the secret of their success. "We didn't try and change each other, did we, love?" Jim said, matter-of-factly. Amy just smiled at him and said, "No, we didn't, did we?"

When the village heard the terrible news that Amy had been diagnosed with cancer at the relatively young age of sixty, a real sense of shock passed through us. We were even more shaken when, within a few short weeks, she died.

The village rallied round Jim, doing the best it could to help him. But, in truth, there was little we could do. In the weeks and months following Amy's death, it was as if he had disappeared.

While Amy was alive, he had been a familiar face walking up and down the road, always ready for a chat. Now he suddenly became invisible. He was no longer seen in the shop, the church or the pub. I walked past Jim's house on an almost daily basis, taking my children, Tony and Ellie, to and from the stop where the school taxi collected and dropped them off. The curtains were always drawn. There was never a sound, even of a radio or television. The only sign that Jim was still living there was the garden. Nobody ever saw him out in the garden, yet its lawns were perfectly manicured, its blooms fit for the Chelsea Flower Show. He must be gardening at night or at crack of dawn, we concluded.

One afternoon, during the summer holidays, a couple of years after Amy's death, Ellie arrived home full of beans.

"I've been talking to Mr Moss," she said.

I knew that a child can sometimes be a healing influence on people who are nursing a terrible loss. Their innocence is an antidote to the despair. I was quietly pleased that Ellie had made contact with Jim so left her to it.

A few days later the subject came up again.

"Mr Moss is such a nice man," Ellie announced. "I told him that he needed a dog."

"Why did you do that?" I wondered.

"He's sad living on his own, isn't he? Nobody should be alone."

A few days later, Ellie came in to announce that Mr Moss had come round to her idea.

"He'd like a dog and wants to talk to you about it," she said.

The next day I popped round to see him.

He came to the door and ushered me in. It only took a second to see how terribly he was missing Amy. The house was immaculate, everything sparkled as if it was new. A large photograph of Amy had taken pride of place in the living room. Standing next to it was a vase of fresh flowers from the garden.

"Is my daughter badgering you to get a dog?" I asked him.

"No, no," he said. "In fact, I think she might be right, I do need a dog." At that time, I had a half dozen dogs, mainly English springer spaniels. "I've seen you with your lovely springers and they seem such good dogs."

We talked about the pros and cons of owning a dog. He understood that it was a big responsibility. I knew he was a cautious man and wasn't going to take any rash decisions. I invited him round to my house, to spend some time with my dogs and see if he got on with them.

"That would be nice," he said. "I'll pop round later in the week."

As it happened, my pack had recently expanded. I'd sold one of my springer spaniels, Ben, to a couple from Sheffield a year earlier. They'd been delighted with him, but then they'd had some bad luck. The husband had a terrible fall and broke his back. They rang me to tell me they could no longer provide him with the active life he needed.

"Would you have him back?" they asked.

I agreed immediately, but I knew I couldn't keep him long term and would have to find a good, new home for him.

Two days after I'd been round to see Jim, he appeared at my front door. I asked him in for a cup of tea, and we sat there talking about dogs. My pack were playing in the garden and I asked them into the kitchen.

It was then that something uncanny happened.

As soon as he arrived in the house, Ben went straight over to Jim and sat down on the floor next to him. Within seconds, Jim was almost instinctively stroking Ben's neck and head.

"What's his name?" he asked.

"That's Ben," I said, deliberately avoiding going into any detail.

As we chatted, Jim kept stroking Ben. And the more he stroked him, the closer Ben snuggled up to him. It was a joy to behold.

Jim left after an hour or so, seeming to have enjoyed himself.

"See you soon, Jan," he said as he headed off.

A couple of days later, Ellie, Tony and I were walking back from the school taxi drop-off. As we went past Jim's house, he was in the window looking out and beckoned to me to wait.

"Glad I caught you, Jan," he said, emerging from the front door. "I've given it a lot of thought and I think I'd like a dog."

"Oh, good for you," I said. "Have you decided on what breed you'd like?"

"Well, if I could find a dog like your Ben, I'd be delighted."

Ellie shot me a look immediately, but she didn't need to say anything.

"Would you like Ben?" I asked.

Jim was taken aback for a moment or two. "Well, I, er," he spluttered, not sure what to say.

Finally, I thought it was the right time to tell him Ben's story. As I explained the situation, Jim's face lit up.

"Jan, I'd love to have him," he beamed.

Even then, I didn't want to foist on Jim a dog that wasn't right for him. So the moment I got home, I put Ben on a lead and walked him round to Jim's house.

"I'll leave you two together for a couple of hours, to see how you get along here," I said. "I'll be back to take Ben home later."

I returned after I'd put the children to bed. I found Ben, snuggled up next to Jim's armchair, looking every inch as if he was another piece of furniture.

"So, Jan, could Ben stay?" he asked simply, stroking Ben once more.

I thought he meant overnight, and so I explained that I didn't think it would be good for Ben, especially as he'd just got over the upheaval of moving back from Sheffield.

"Oh, not just for tonight. Can he stay for good?" Jim said.

Ben was sitting at Jim's feet now. The pair of them looked as if they were made for each other. I couldn't help myself as the tears started rolling down my face.

"Of course he can, Jim," I said, when I had eventually regained a little of my composure. "I can't think of anywhere else I'd rather he stayed."

The transformation was miraculous. About a week after Ben had moved in with Jim, I met a lady in the village shop.

"I haven't seen Jim Moss for two years, now I've seen him every day this week," she said.

Almost immediately, Jim had become one of the familiar sights in the village, striding along with Ben on his lead. Once a week, he and Ben would walk four miles to the nearest market town, where Jim would pop into a pub for a couple of drinks, then do his shopping at the market and walk back home again. He was once more the man he had been before Amy's death — only now it was he and Ben who were inseparable.

It was many months later that I finally got to have a proper talk with Jim. I saw him in the village and he invited me in for a cup of tea and a chat.

The atmosphere in the house had changed completely from when I had last been there. Before, it was clear that everything was pretty much as it had been when Amy was alive. The house looked as if a woman lived in it — there were knick-knacks and feminine touches everywhere. Now it was very different. Amy hadn't been forgotten — her picture still dominated the living room, and the flowers were as fresh as ever — but the rest of the house now reflected Jim's personality rather than hers. He had redecorated and bought new furniture. The knick-knacks had gone and another photograph took pride of place on Jim's mantelpiece — a lovely portrait of Ben.

Jim was obviously in the mood to talk and, as the tea flowed, he explained how important Ben had been to him. He confirmed what had been obvious to all of us who knew him. For the first two years after Amy's death, he'd been a lost soul.

"I hadn't been able to come to terms with losing Amy. I couldn't let go of her because I was all alone," he said. Ben's arrival had provided him with company — and the strength finally to let go.

"I hadn't been able to grieve properly until I had him," he said. "When Ben arrived, I was able to start crying. He didn't laugh at me for doing it, or stumble for the right words to console me. He just sidled up close and was there for me. That dog gave me a reason to live again," he told me. "Ben showed me my life wasn't over."

As so often happens, the dog had opened new doors for Jim. For some reason, people are more likely to strike up a conversation with someone who is walking a dog. And so it proved with Jim.

"Ben has helped me make a lot of new friends," Jim explained. He told me his life was busier than it had ever been.

It was almost overwhelming to hear just how profound an effect this dog had had on Jim's life.

Jim and Ben's story has always remained with me, and it is an important one for a number of reasons. I am often asked to sum up what is so rewarding about having a dog. To be honest, it's something I often find hard to put into words. On many an occasion I have used Jim's story as the answer. To me, their story says more about the pleasures of owning a dog than any worthy, wordy statement. Jim and Ben were there for each other when it really mattered. And they rewarded each other with all the loyalty and love they could muster. I often think of the two of them walking down the country lanes together. If there's an image of owner and dog in perfect harmony, then that's it.

In the years that followed, as I delved deeper into our relationship with dogs, I came to realise he symbolised something more significant. Jim, as far as I was aware, wasn't someone with experience of living with dogs. Yet, as I'd seen from the moment he and Ben had first met, he seemed to have a natural affinity, they seemed to trust and like him. When Ben had gone to live with him, they had built up a remarkably close bond. And again it seemed to have happened quite naturally. Jim never once came to me for any additional advice on looking after springers. I never heard of Jim attending any of the obedience classes that were popular in the area at the time. He just got on with it — with admirable results.

It was only years later, when I thought about that conversation with him, that it struck me what the key to his success must have been. It came to me when I remembered Jim with Amy all those years before. He had approached his relationship with Ben just as he had treated his marriage to Amy. When Amy had been alive, Jim had respected her. As he'd said himself, he hadn't tried to change her, to mould her into something she was not. He had let her be herself — and she'd let him be himself.

Essentially, he had done the same thing with Ben. Jim had let his dog be himself and Ben had rewarded his master by allowing him to be himself at a time when he desperately needed to do so. With Ben around, Jim

36

had finally felt free to cry openly and mourn. It was something so natural, yet at the same time so rare.

Of course, as we all know, relationships are not always this simple. Ordinary life can be much more complicated and demanding than this. People do have to change and make allowances for each other — and their dogs have to fit into their life as well. But within Jim and Ben's story is an essential truth — something that has struck me as more and more important as the years have gone by: respect is the key to all great relationships.

FEELING THE FORCE

The importance of drawing on the lessons of others

Formulating the ideas that make up my method of communicating with dogs was a slow, almost imperceptible, invisible process. There was no real eureka moment, no apples fell from the trees. For years, usually without my realising it, people or events provided me with pieces in a giant jigsaw puzzle. Then one day I looked down to see that jigsaw complete.

The short version of the story is this. As my involvement in the dog world grew through the 1970s and 1980s, I had begun to harbour a deep distrust of traditional training methods. I attended — and even ran — my fair share of classes promoting these views, but I felt more and more that they were too aggressive, too reliant on the domination of the owner and the subjugation of the dog to his or her will. I felt there had to be another way.

The turning point came early in the 1990s, when fate conspired to take me by the hand. It was then that I saw a demonstration by the American "horse whisperer" Monty Roberts. It was an inspiration to see the way he invited the horses to follow him of their own free will, using signals that the animals understood instinctively, rather than resorting to violence or aggressive behaviour of any sort. Monty and his "join up" method set me thinking about whether it was possible to replicate this in dogs, to connect once more with the lost language that man and his best friend shared thousands of years ago.

While I had always been interested in dogs, by now I had begun to see them and their behaviour in a broader historical context, specifically in terms of their relationship with their ancient ancestor, the wolf.

I had discovered that wolf packs operate according to a strict hierarchy, with the Alpha pair as leaders and sole decision makers and the remainder of the pack ranked below according to a strict pecking order. Studying films and documentaries about wolves, I saw that the Alpha pair used four key moments in the day-to-day life of the pack to assert and sometimes reassert their authority. At mealtimes, for instance, they would always eat first. When it was time to go on the hunt, the Alpha pair would lead. At times of perceived danger, the Alphas would either withdraw the pack to safety or confront the threat on their behalf. And, finally, when the pack was reunited after a separation of some kind, the subordinates would pay the Alpha pair some kind of homage, licking frantically at their faces and carrying their bodies and tails lower than their leaders.

At the time, I had a pack of highly intelligent and responsive dogs sharing my life. As I studied the way they interacted more closely, I was surprised to see my own pack indulged in its share of ritualistic behaviour too. Like all dogs, they misbehaved here and there, but they also seemed to do so in a repetitive way, as if there was a pattern to it. As I watched them more closely, I saw striking similarities to the behaviour within the wolf packs. I realised my dogs became most agitated at mealtimes, as we prepared for our walks, when visitors arrived at the house and on my return from work in the evenings. What was more, they interacted with each other in a way that suggested there was a pecking order between them. For instance, my German shepherd, Sasha, seemed to carry herself in a more erect way, as if to keep a distance from the rest of the pack. At other times, she would interact with the rest of the pack, often licking them in a ritualised way. Clearly, the dog had been taken out of the wolf pack, but the wolf pack hadn't been taken out of the dog. I began to see that my dogs were operating according to the same, hard-wired instincts as their ancestors. There was some kind of hierarchy within the pack and their behaviour was being coloured by it.

The real breakthrough came when I realised they were treating me as part of the pack. At the time, my dogs jumped up at me when I came home, pulled at the lead whenever we went out on a walk, and barked and became agitated when people appeared unexpectedly at the door. I began to wonder whether my dogs believed I too was part of their hierarchy — and whether they saw me as a subordinate member within our pack. Just because I saw myself as being the person responsible for looking after our domestic pack, it didn't mean that they shared that view. Suddenly, all sorts of behaviours were explained. If my dogs believed they were responsible for me, for instance, the causes of separation anxiety became clear. It was no longer a case of a dog pining for its owner when they were not at home, but one of a frantic parent desperate because it had lost its child and had no idea whether it was safe or not. If there was a eureka moment, then that was the closest I've come to it.

From there I began to see that the key to changing my relationship with my dogs lay in removing the mantle of leadership from them and taking it on myself. What was particularly appealing about this was that if I could do this naturally, by using signals that they instinctively understood, they would relinquish this responsibility automatically, they would elect me leader of their own free will. There would be no need for violence, coercion or subjugation. The dogs would simply be listening to their instincts. What's more, as long as I remained a convincing Alpha, they would follow my lead — again as their instincts told them to.

Slowly, falteringly at first, I began to put together a system of signals, to be used at the four key times so that I could establish myself as leader of my own domestic pack. When we reunited after a separation I made sure we did so on my terms and at a time of my choosing, as a leader would do. I did this by ignoring any attention-seeking, waiting until the dogs calmed down, then calling them to me. In a similar vein I made sure the dogs were calm before leading them out on our walks. At the same time, I began to take charge of situations when there was a perceived danger to the pack. Here, if the dogs barked or got excited at the sign of a visitor at the door, I simply thanked them for alerting me to the danger, thereby relieving them of the responsibility of worrying. Finally, I took charge of mealtimes, taking a mouthful of a snack before laying down the food for my dogs to eat. Again, the idea was that if I was in control of the food then I must be the leader of the domestic pack. Throughout the process, I underscored everything with positive reinforcement, using food rewards to help speed the message that if they did the right thing, good things happened.

It was like watching a minor miracle take place. Over the following weeks and months, I was able to watch as our levels of communication improved beyond all recognition. And their behaviour improved enormously too — as did my enjoyment of life with them. One thing led to another, and soon I found myself using my method to help other people overcome problems with their dogs. By the mid 1990s, I had taken my first tentative steps into full-time "troubleshooting", with my own small business.

It was an exhilarating period in my life. What made it all the more exciting was the way it crystallised some of the important lessons I'd been given earlier in my life. I began to see that in my earlier life I had been given many pointers as to the way ahead. Encounters I had forgotten in the past suddenly began to take on new meanings. The respect I already felt for those wise voices of my youth now grew deeper than ever.

I saw, for instance, the wisdom of old heads such as my Uncle Jim and how right he was in believing we should go along with an animal's instincts, and to trust its nature to show us the right way to do things. By adopting this philosophy with my own dogs, I had been shown the way ahead. I understood the significance of what Jim Moss had taught me about respecting your dog — and the rewards that flowed from that. I saw too the importance of my cousin Doreen's idea that dogs have feelings.

At the root of my new-found thinking about how best to get dogs to comply with my wishes, was the idea of dogs' innate selfishness, the "What's in It for Me" principle, as illustrated by Uncle George as he persuaded Rex to stay off his rose beds. Now, here I was using the idea that it is far better to work with the dog than against it, using positive reinforcement to underline key messages.

I had gleaned so much from listening and watching other people and their dogs. But as I began to use my new-found knowledge, I was certain there was plenty more to learn, both from the present and the past. And I wasn't wrong.

LIVING IN THE REAL WORLD

Why great owners know their limits

It goes without saying that most owners want the best for their dogs. It is the most natural thing in the world to want to provide your pet with as happy, contented and fulfilling a life as you possibly can. Yet life, as we all know, is never that straightforward. We have our dreams but real life has a habit of getting in the way of them and when that happens, we are faced with some stark choices.

In my view, the way owners respond to the realities of dog ownership defines them as clearly as anything else. The really great owners I've met have all had a strong sense of the limitations they face. I have come across many outstanding people in this respect, but few were more impressive than Terry and Sandra, a couple I met at the very beginning of my career as a "dog listener".

Terry and Sandra lived in a village near the Humber Bridge, a short drive from my home back in the 1990s, the small town of Winterton, in North Lincolnshire.

They had been having severe problems with their crossbred dog Guinness and had heard of me from friends in the area. "We're very concerned about him," Terry said when he telephoned me. "If we can't improve his behaviour we're afraid it's going to end badly."

When I went to visit them, I was still working full time for the local social services department. I had formulated my method and had helped a few people improve their dogs' behaviour, but the idea of doing it professionally had not really occurred to me. My encounter with Guinness almost persuaded me to give up before I'd really started.

Terry and Sandra had got Guinness from a rescue centre, where he'd arrived as one of three abandoned puppies. When he first moved in at the age of ten weeks, he had been lively but manageable. Now, at the age of two and a half, Guinness was a giant of a dog. He must have weighed ten stone and was so massive you could have put a saddle on him. He was one of the most obvious examples of an Alpha Male dog I had ever encountered. No one was going to tell him what to do.

Terry and Sandra reeled off incident after incident in which Guinness had refused to listen to them. If they told him to sit, he would stand there looking at them with disdain written all over his face. If they told him to leave a room he would stand firm. When he was younger, Terry had been able physically to remove him. He was now so big and powerful, even that option was no longer available.

He was equally stubborn when he wanted something from them. Guinness would routinely take hold of Terry or Sandra's trouser leg or shirtsleeve and try to drag them in the direction of whatever it was he wanted. Their protests were usually in vain and both had got used to caving in.

They had both owned dogs in the past and knew this was a situation that just couldn't go on. But nothing they did seemed to help. Guinness had been taken to training classes locally but he had grabbed the trainer's arm with such force they were told he was "too stupid" to be trained. Terry and Sandra were loving owners and they thought the world of Guinness. But he was already aggressive towards strangers, squaring up to them and barking loudly in their faces and their concern was that this defiance was leading in only one direction.

"It's only a matter of time before he does something worse — and that will be the end of him," Terry told me.

The success I had helping other people with their dogs had given me some confidence that I could help. My method was based on the idea that dogs' problems stem from their mistaken belief that they are the leader of their domestic pack and that their owners contribute to this by behaving as if they are indeed subordinate members of that pack. The only way to correct this was by getting the owner to replace the dog at the head of the domestic hierarchy by means of a bloodless coup, using a visual language the dog can understand to get the message across. This was something that would be implemented gradually at the four key moments in the pack's daily routine — when they reunited after separation, at times of perceived danger, at mealtimes and when out on the walk. I would begin the process myself during my visit, but after that it would be up to the owner to keep it going over the days, weeks, months (and even years!) ahead.

There was no question in my mind that Guinness saw himself as leader. Even when speaking to Terry on the phone, I had immediately known what the disdainful look he described was all about. It was Guinness' way of saying: "Excuse me, who are *you*, telling *me* what to do?" The way he gave me a similar look when I arrived at the house only confirmed this.

After I'd explained what I wanted to do, we began the difficult job of "trading places", relieving Guinness of the job of leader and installing Terry and Sandra in his place. This was easier said than done.

We began by simply ignoring him, as an Alpha would naturally dismiss a subordinate in its pack in order to assert itself. Guinness clearly wasn't going to have this and he began doing what he could to get our attention. First, he began tugging at Terry's trousers. When I asked Terry to block him from doing this, he then started barking in their faces, licking their hands, doing anything he could think of to get their attention. When he saw they were ignoring him, he pulled his bed from another room and placed it in the middle of the living room, only to have Sandra remove it immediately at my request.

Dogs are extremely smart and it was a measure of how intelligent Guinness was and how hard he was thinking about things, that a lot of this behaviour was completely new to Terry and Sandra. The key was not to acknowledge this. Every nerve end in their bodies was telling them to acknowledge him and tell him off, but — encouraged by me — they stuck at it and refused to recognise any of this. This went on for almost an hour, during which time Guinness grew, if anything, even more determined. After a while Terry and Sandra were finding it really hard so I suggested we move to another room. No sooner had we shut the door behind us than Guinness was pulling at the door handle and trying to get in.

It was very hard work, but after an hour and a half, our perseverance paid off and Guinness became noticeably calmer. By the time I left the house the attention-seeking behaviour had ceased. I knew there was a long way to go, but I was hopeful they'd made a good start.

I left them to it, but asked them to stay in touch if there were difficulties. Over the course of the following week, I heard from them on a daily basis. Guinness had calmed down a little and was behaving less manically when they ignored him. But problems arose whenever they went to reward him.

Terry loved playing with Guinness. To him there was nothing more fun than lying on the floor and treating his dog to a bit of rough-and-tumble wrestling or throwing a stick around in the park. But these were precisely the sort of signals that had to be avoided. As I told Terry, Guinness couldn't play the game until he knew the rules. And he was showing no signs of understanding them, nor would he while Terry was effectively paying homage to Guinness as leader. He had made progress, but the reality was that Guinness' leadership instincts were so powerful, it only needed the slightest false signal for him to forget all he'd been taught and to resume power once more. Any sign of the old affection or warmth from Terry or Sandra sent Guinness into a real flip. He would jump up, begin barking and generally revert to his old ways almost immediately. It was as if he was a deposed political leader, unable to accept his removal from power and desperate to take over again.

Terry understood that he had to adopt a colder, more detached manner with Guinness, but he was finding it hard to do so. "It seems so formal. I want to play with him, I want to show him I love him," he said.

This was a comment I heard a lot. For most people, ruffling a dog's coat or giving him a squeeze is one of the most natural and instinctive acts in the world. I knew this only too well for myself. Yet I also knew how important it was to remain in control, to display the aloof, slightly detached demeanour of the leader of the pack. So my response to this had already become well established. "I know how natural it feels to show love to a dog, and you are not going to stop doing that. You're just going to channel it in another way, turn that affection in a different direction," I told Terry.

Terry understood the risks if he didn't stick to the method. "It's tough, but I'll persevere," he said.

It was probably three months or so before I heard from them again. This time Terry and Sandra sounded much more positive. They were making great progress, Guinness was going out for long walks, he was behaving much better around visitors and — most importantly of all — he was doing what Terry and Sandra asked of him.

They had learned to reward him in a matter-of-fact way, with a "good lad" and a stroke of the head rather than the ruffles and cuddles of the past. It was a sacrifice worth making, they said.

It was about a year later that I saw them next. I happened to be in their village and thought I'd pop in. Terry answered the door and was soon joined by Guinness, who approached him in a very controlled, self-disciplined way. When I asked how they were getting on I sensed a hint of sadness in his voice.

"We're OK," Terry said.

I was still uncertain of where I was going with my method — if anywhere — and I really needed the feedback.

"Please tell me if you're not convinced we've done the right thing or if it's not worked. I need to know," I said.

"Oh no, it's worked, Guinness is a different dog these days," Terry said. "What breaks my heart is that I can't get close to him."

Terry called him over, stroked his head and said "good boy". "That's as much as we can do without him going back to his old ways," he said.

50

As ever, they had not been short of advice from friends and family. Many had said they were wrong to adopt such a "way out" method. But whenever anyone had sounded off, Terry had challenged them to do better.

He had simply let them call Guinness over, shower him with cuddles and then watch him revert to his former, uncontrollable self. On one occasion, his brother had criticised what Terry was doing as "cruel".

"I told him he was free to have a go, but within ten seconds Guinness had jumped at him, knocked him over and pinned him to the floor," Terry said. "It was the only way I could get the message through to them," he told me with a resigned smile.

There were consolations. Terry and Sandra loved walking and were now able to go on long rambles with Guinness. He was now very responsive to their requests and behaved impeccably when he came into contact with other people or dogs, allowing Terry and Sandra to relax and enjoy themselves much more when they were out together.

"I still have to stop myself picking up a stick and throwing it though," Terry said, the regret unmistakeable in his voice. "But I accept it. I know it will set him back into his old ways. Nobody else is going to do this for him, it's our responsibility and it's up to us to look after him."

In some ways theirs is a sad story. Even now, years later, and armed with much more experience and knowledge, I honestly don't think there would have been an alternative solution to Guinness' problems. He was such a powerful dog, the signals required to get the message through to him had to be powerful and unequivocal too. He needed to be managed very carefully.

Yet, theirs is also an inspirational story, one that has stayed with me over the years. In really difficult circumstances, Terry and Sandra did something of which they could be very proud. They had wanted something else from their dog, but they'd accepted the reality — it wasn't possible. Rather than abandoning him, they'd been big enough and brave enough to accept these limitations and build their life with him on that basis. I'm sure they both learned something in doing so. It certainly taught me something priceless.

When I first ventured out into the world with my ideas about how to improve our relationship with dogs, my greatest concern was that I was in a minority. I had been unsure whether many people shared my passionate feelings for dogs and anyone actually cared for them the same way. I had seen more than my share of bad owners. More worrying in a way, I knew there were many, many people to whom their dog was a minor priority, something to be enjoyed as long as it didn't require too much effort or thought.

The method I had evolved was simple, yet it required a great deal of thought and hard work. Since I had begun working with owners, I had become assailed by doubts. Was I living in cloud cuckoo land? Would I find many owners willing to put in that graft and make the sacrifice sometimes necessary to make their relation-ship with their dog work? Terry and Sandra provided me with my answer. At a time when I needed to see it, they showed me that there were people in the world who were prepared to go as far as necessary, and to live within whatever limitations necessary to make their pet happy. It was a humbling — but also hugely encouraging — lesson. And I'm always grateful to them for having provided it.

ROLE MODELS

Why great owners lead by example

The more I developed my ideas, the more I realised how important it is to project the right kind of leadership. Through studying wolves and working with my own dogs, I had learned that dogs don't associate leadership with ranting and raving, bullying and dictating or even overt affection. Instead, natural leaders seemed to demonstrate calmness, consistency and decisiveness. As I developed these principles, I realised that I had seen them applied before by another inspiring owner.

Throughout my life I have met people whose ideas about our relationship with dogs have influenced me almost subliminally. I have not felt their full impact until long after the event.

Back in the 1970s, for instance, I had had no idea how important my friendship with the headmistress of our local primary school would become. It is only now, thirty years on, that I can fully appreciate the lesson Patsy and her German shepherd, Bracken, provided.

The idea that children could receive a better education in the countryside had been a key influence in our decision to leave London for rural Lincolnshire. In London, classrooms were overcrowded and teachers overstretched even then.

In contrast, living in the small village of Firsby, I had a choice of two excellent schools for our children, Tony and Ellie. One was within a mile of our home, the other was three and a half miles away. I wasn't going to let convenience alone dictate which of the two Tony and Ellie attended, so I looked at both, comparing the schools from varying perspectives. Naturally, I looked at the available statistics and asked local people for their opinions. Finally, I decided to get some evidence of my own and spent a couple of mornings sitting outside first one school then the other, simply watching the pupils and their parents arriving.

As everyone had predicted, the school closest to us seemed a decent enough place. It had a good reputation for exam results and people spoke well of matters such as discipline and homework, but as I watched the children and their parents filing in, their heads slightly bowed, there seemed to be something lacking. It was only when I visited the second school that I saw what it was.

This school was in an old Victorian building in the village of Thorpe St Peter. There were only thirty children there, divided up into two classes. But there was something noticeably different about it. As I sat outside, I saw children skipping and running to the gates with a smile on their faces. At the entrance there were teachers greeting them with warm faces and jolly "good mornings". It seemed a happier, friendlier place

— precisely the sort of environment I wanted for Tony and Ellie. And it didn't take me long to realise that the person most responsible for creating the school's atmosphere was the headmistress, Patsy.

Patsy was a warm lady in her forties. The first clue I got that she was something special came a few days after my son Tony had started in the infants' class and she rang me out of the blue one evening. For a split second I panicked, convinced there was a problem with my child. But she quickly calmed my nerves.

"I hope you don't mind my calling you at this hour, but I just wanted to tell you that your son gave me one of the nicest teaching experiences I've had in a long time today," she said. She went on to explain how he'd responded really well to a word game she'd been playing with him that morning. To me, it was a shock that such teachers even existed. It seemed like fate had directed us towards her.

Over the following weeks, months and years, I got to know her well, mainly through my involvement with the school, where I joined in fund-raising events, helped with an art class and worked with Patsy making costumes for the annual pantomime. As we got to know each other better, I became a regular visitor to her house, adjacent to the school, where she lived with her husband George, her son and a beautiful big German shepherd called Bracken.

As I mentioned earlier, then, even more than now, German shepherds had an undeserved reputation as dangerous dogs. In truth, this was largely because at the time very few people owned bigger, more physical breeds like Akitas, Dobermans or Rottweilers. As the only "big bad dog" most British people knew of, it was inevitable that the German shepherd got all the bad press — even I was in awe of them at the time. Much as I loved dogs, I would never have conceived of owning a German shepherd. I simply didn't think I was up to the job. Bracken was the first one to make me consider changing my mind.

Physically, he was a giant, a really intimidating-looking dog. Yet in terms of personality Bracken was the most good-natured, unthreatening dog you could have wished to meet.

Patsy's side door opened on to the school playground, where Bracken would occasionally play during term time. Patsy was always careful not to let him out when the schoolyard was full. Because of their reputations, many children and their parents were simply terrified of German shepherds and would freeze or, even worse, scream at the sight of them. But occasionally Patsy would let Bracken play there under supervision — and if ever there was a dog to break the standard perception of German shepherds it was Bracken. He would let children touch and stroke him and would even play with them at times. There was never any hint of trouble.

Given the way everyone else got on with Bracken, it was all the more surprising to discover that Patsy's husband George wasn't quite so fond of him. Indeed, the more I got to know him, the more puzzling it became.

George, it turned out, had been a world-renowned breeder of German shepherds for use as security dogs in the armed forces. He had supplied dogs all around the world, breeding them at a terrific rate. One year, he told me, he had provided three hundred puppies for forces as far afield as Australia, South Africa and Canada.

It wasn't hard to spot that he'd served in the army himself. He had the bearing of a sergeant major and had the booming voice to go with it. When he spoke, he did so in one of only two volumes — loud and deafening. Talking to him, I learned that he had applied the same rigid, military-style discipline in breeding and training his dogs. "They were there to do a job, a tough job, and that's what I prepared them for," he would say.

Almost immediately I got to know them, it was clear that George and Patsy had very, very different relationships with Bracken. Patsy and I spent many an evening or afternoon making Prince Charming or Widow Twanky outfits for the school pantomime. Whenever we did so, Bracken would lie down alongside us, gently nuzzling his head against Patsy. Yet the minute George appeared he would either run behind the sofa or out of the room.

Not long before, George had had a German shepherd of his own, Bracken's father, Dale. When Dale had died Patsy had expected him to get another dog. But with his health fading, George — very responsibly — had decided against it. "I'm not fit enough to look after a German shepherd any more," he said.

In Dale's absence, at the least you might have expected George to form a bond with Bracken. He was Dale's son, after all. But rather than bringing them closer, Dale's passing drove them apart. To George, Bracken wasn't a patch on his father. Whenever he ran away from him, George would say things like, "Where's Mr Wimpy off to now?" or "A lot of use that dog would be in the army." On one occasion he said, "Dale would have defended me with his life. That one would just run for his life."

George clearly blamed Bracken's personality on the approach Patsy had taken with his training. In preparing his army dogs, George made no bones about the fact that he traded on domination and fear, on being forceful and authoritarian. "A dog's got to know who's in charge," he would say. So if a dog defied him, he showed him who was boss through physical action, a pull on a chain, a shout or even a smack. "It's the only way," George would say.

Patsy, on the other hand, had trained Bracken in a more gentle way, spending long hours in the garden teaching him to sit and come, to fetch and retrieve balls. To my eyes at least, she had succeeded brilliantly. But to George she had only succeeded in producing a dog that was weak and — to his eyes — almost an embarrassment. Whenever he saw Patsy being affectionate with Bracken he would say things like: "You're too soft with that dog" and "It's no wonder he's a wimp, the way you treat him."

I never saw George being violent towards Bracken — in truth, he never had the chance. Whenever he came

59

anywhere near the dog, Bracken made himself scarce. The way he disappeared like this seemed to irritate George in itself. If he complained, however, Patsy gave him short shrift. "The dog doesn't like loud noises," she would say. George's response was to call him a "coward".

Neither of us could deny that George's ideas had worked for him. To have built the reputation he had and keep it for as long as he did, must have taken a lot of hard work and professionalism. But the training method he used was not something that sat comfortably with me. I imagined his dogs must have been largely unhappy, rather frightened creatures.

I'm sure Patsy knew what I was thinking. I'd often catch Patsy's eye when he said cruel things. She'd be standing there saying nothing, a gentle, knowing smile on her face. It was a smile that said: "Don't worry, my way works, and I'm sticking to it."

At the time, I wasn't aware that I was learning anything. It was only over a period of years that things began to sink in. Patsy's attitude towards Bracken exactly reflected her approach to the children she taught at school.

Patsy was one of the most remarkable teachers I encountered during my children's education. First and foremost she had a real presence about her, a way of carrying herself that made the children pay attention without her really having to say very much at all. It was, I suppose, an air of authority — but it was an air she wore lightly, benignly. She also had a gift for treating each and every one of her pupils as an individual. I remember being in the classroom on one occasion when she was talking to the mother of a boy called David, the youngest of three brothers at the school. "He's not like his brothers, I'm afraid," the mother said, implying he wasn't as bright as his siblings.

"He's not his brothers, he's David," Patsy chastised her.

These qualities were as obvious at Patsy's home as they were in the classroom. At home, George would regularly compare Bracken unfavourably with his father Dale. "You wouldn't think he's his father's son," he'd say. "He would never have cut it in the forces."

Patsy would simply smile and say gently: "He's not his father's son, he's himself." Nothing more.

My interest in dogs was increasing hugely at the time. I had some springers and was enjoying some modest success on the show front. I had often thought about asking Patsy directly about George and Bracken, but had bottled out of it each time.

Then one afternoon, we were working on some outfits for a school production. Bracken had been lying next to her as usual, but when George had come into the room Bracken bolted to hide behind the sofa. When George disappeared again and Bracken sidled back up alongside her, I summoned up the courage at last.

"I hope you don't mind me saying this, but I've noticed Bracken gets very anxious around George," I said.

"Well, George has his ideas about how a dog should be handled — and I have mine," she said with an ironic arch of an eyebrow.

61

"But he's the expert, he's the one with all the experience. Why don't you agree with him?" I asked.

She thought for a moment, then gave me one of those gentle, reassuring smiles of hers.

"Look at it this way, Jan," she said. "Imagine if I treated the children the way George treats dogs. Do you think I'd get the best out of them if I did that?"

My face obviously told the story.

"No, of course not," Patsy said before I could reply. "I think the way to get the best out of children is to encourage them. Of course, you have to have rules, but that doesn't mean you can't have fun as well," she went on. "I think it's the same for any creature. I get the best out of Bracken by encouraging him to do things, not by bullying him the way George thinks I should."

Patsy was an enlightening influence in all sorts of ways. She taught me a great deal about German shepherds, and was probably responsible for implanting in me the belief that one day I might be good enough to have one. (In that sense, I owe her a debt beyond words because without her I wouldn't have got Sasha, the dog that did most to lead me to the discovery of my method.)

But within that comment lay the most profound thing Patsy taught me. It was an extension of what my cousin Doreen had told me when I was a child. Patsy too was considering the question she posed all the time: "How would you feel if someone treated you like that?" But her lesson ran deeper. In one sense George was right — dogs did need leaders. What Patsy understood was that there was a big difference between leadership and dictatorship.

Years later, as I developed my method, I saw the immense benefits that flowed from persuading dogs to do things without recourse to violence or aggression, of their own free will. At the same time, I saw how much this relied on providing the right kind of leadership. The parallels with humans struck me clearly. The great leaders of history, the people that have really commanded respect and inspired their followers, were not violent, terrifying tyrants like Saddam Hussein and Stalin, but the calm, decisive, consistent yet inspiring figures, like Gandhi and Nelson Mandela. Today, when I pass on my method to owners, I stress the huge importance of replicating these qualities. I ask owners to use confident body language and be decisive and authoritative. But I also emphasise the need to speak sparingly — only when they have something to say — and underline the importance of remaining calm, consistent and convincing at all times.

I can see now that Patsy embodied each and every one of these qualities. Somewhere, deep in the recesses of my mind, she stimulated a line of thinking that bore fruit in the most unexpected ways.

Thirty years ago, I thought she was one of the most exceptional people I'd met in my life. Today, my opinion of her, not just as a teacher but as a person and a dog owner, is, if anything, even higher.

SECOND AMONG EQUALS

Why great owners always put their dogs first

We live in self-centred times, an age when many people put themselves first and — even worse — see themselves as "victims" when the rest of the world doesn't place them on a pedestal. It probably sounds very old-fashioned saying this, but the virtues of duty, loyalty, sacrifice and selflessness that I grew up with seem to have been consigned to the past. I do think this is one of the subtler, more subliminal reasons why so many people are drawn to dogs — creatures for whom all those positive, old-fashioned qualities are purely instinctive.

In general, dog owners tend to share these qualities too. There are, of course, exceptions, but in my experience the best owners are those who put their own welfare second to that of their dog. I'm sure many of us feel we do this. We are all willing to put ourselves out to help our dogs, particularly in times of need. In the course of my work with dogs, I have learned a lot about just how selfless people can really be. No owners were more instructive than two ladies, Una and Renate.

★ ★ ★

The sacrifice Una made was unique because when I met her she wasn't even an owner. That, however, is the whole point of her story. Una attended one of the courses I run at my home in Lincolnshire. She was a widow, in her mid-fifties, getting ready for early retirement. She'd loved dogs since she was a little girl and had had many over the years. But, for the past fourteen years, she'd fought the urge to have one because of her work. She was a teacher, deeply involved with her school and working long hours. Given the demands of her professional life, she felt it wasn't right for her to have a dog.

It was a stand I applauded wholeheartedly. Personally, I don't think anyone who works full time should have a dog, unless they've got a dog walker to give them exercise and attention during the day. But, as I got talking to Una, the full extent of her sacrifice became clear. In the circumstances she'd been through, many people would have given in to their desire for a dog to share their life. That she hadn't done so was an act of exceptional selflessness.

She had been married to an architect, with whom she had three children. They had lived a happy family life — and had a succession of Labradors, acquiring them as puppies. Their children had reached university age when their lives were changed irretrievably. Una's husband had been diagnosed with a terminal disease. She had faced the awful job of nursing him through his long and painful decline. I could empathise with her entirely since it was something I'd been through myself with my father, a decade or so earlier. Watching

65

someone you love suffering is an awful experience. If it hadn't been for my dogs I would have struggled to cope at all.

But this was not an emotional support that Una would have available to her for long. By the time her husband's illness was diagnosed, the last of their Labradors was ageing. During the final stages of her husband's illness, Una had to break the news to him that the dog had passed on. It devastated both of them. In better times, they would have got a new pup immediately. But Una knew that it wasn't the right time to get another dog. The Labrador had been very elderly and hadn't needed much in the way of exercise so it wasn't too much of a drain on her. But the idea of a puppy was unthinkable in the circumstances.

When her husband passed away, Una admitted her world seemed utterly empty. Again, I understood what she went through from my own experience with my father. She had known he was slipping away, but it was still a huge shock when he finally went. Coming home to an empty home at night was a heartbreaking experience for her.

For a woman who had spent her entire life with dogs, it would have been the most natural thing to get a dog for company. Personally, I don't know whether I would have been able to deny myself the loving companion-ship of a dog at a time like that, even if — like Una — I knew it wasn't right. She, however, was made of sterner stuff. Instead, she poured herself into her work after her husband's death. As well as the normal school duties, she was also involved with the choir and other extracurricular activities. She knew it would be selfish to have a dog, even though every instinct within her cried out for one. Every time she went for a walk in her local park she saw others enjoying the company of their dogs. It was really hard for her.

She carried on like this for two years, but eventually she came up with a solution. Una asked her local animal sanctuary whether she could help out, and they jumped at the offer. These places are always short of willing volunteers, particularly ones with Una's abilities. For the next dozen years, the sanctuary fulfilled all her needs. She would groom, walk and play with the dogs there. Over the years, she brought many of them back to health before seeing them off to good homes. It was good, worthwhile work, and it brought dogs back into Una's life — if not her home — again.

It had been a few months before she came to see me that things had changed. Her husband had left her well provided for. The opportunity for early retirement came up and she took it. Una was sure what she wanted to do. She had got so much pleasure from working with rescue dogs that she had determined to take in two from the sanctuary. Even then, however, she had to delay their arrival for a short time. When her husband had been alive, they had promised themselves a trip to Mexico. Una told me she was going to go there before getting the dogs. After that her travels would be over, and she would be devoted to them.

As I spoke to her during the two days she spent with me on my course, I couldn't help but admire her courage, steadfastness and sheer selflessness. How many other dog lovers would have made that kind of sacrifice? I asked myself.

Una went off on her trip to Mexico and had a fabulous time. She returned to England, ready to begin her new life. She has the dogs now. They must be among the luckiest dogs alive.

Owners like Una are constantly making me rethink my attitude to dogs. No sooner have I encountered a dog lover who, it seems to me, represents the ultimate in dedication than I am encountering another person who has made even greater sacrifices. The bar is always being raised.

Most owners are willing to make such sacrifices for their dogs, of course. And most of us put our dog's welfare at least on a par with our own most of the time. But how many of us would be prepared to sacrifice our own personal happiness for the sake of our dog? How many of us would risk losing the love of our life so as to ensure our pet's welfare? It wasn't long after I had met Una that I met a lady who was ready to do precisely that. Renate, once more, made me raise the bar.

Renate was a very successful career woman. She lived in Scotland, in Aberdeen, but travelled extensively, often spending long secondments in foreign climes. About five years ago she was posted to Portugal. Like so many ex-pats, she found herself living in a large "compound"-style residence. Situated on the outskirts of an old historic town, it was a very comfortable, convivial place, with a large quadrangle in the middle and a real community atmosphere. She enjoyed it enormously.

Sadly, Portugal, like so many Mediterranean countries, has a large number of stray dogs and the residence proved something of a magnet for the town's population. Dogs have an inbuilt radar when it comes to tracking down homes that might provide rich pickings. They would roam the place, scavenging for food or accepting scraps from those residents who felt sorry for them.

Renate wasn't a dog person at all and paid little attention to the compound's canine visitors. A month or so after her arrival there, her neighbours asked her whether she'd be willing to club together with them for the benefit of one of the strays that visited them regularly. She didn't want to seem uncaring or cruel, so listened to what they had to say.

Someone had given the dog the name Def. He was a very well-built crossbreed, like many of the strays there, a German shepherd-type dog. The dog-loving members of the community had taken a real shine to Def — there was something about him that had marked him out as a friendlier, gentler dog than the rest. So they had been upset a few days earlier when he had appeared with a nasty gash on his back leg and almost lame. No one knew how it had got there, whether he'd had an accident, been hit by a car or been in a fight. All they knew was they had to get him to a vet as soon as possible.

Renate made a contribution willingly. A few days later Def was taken to the vets where he was treated. As

69

he recuperated, Def remained in the residence where he became the community dog. He'd sit around in the sunshine, where people would bring him titbits and generally make a fuss. Everyone became really attached to him, including, to her surprise, Renate. Renate didn't think of herself as a dog person. She'd admired dogs here and there, but hadn't really considered having one herself. But there was something about Def that attracted her. She was particularly touched by the fact that he had obviously had a rough life. It didn't really matter that she didn't know what his life had entailed — in many ways she would rather not have known. Without really noticing it, she found herself spending more and more time with him. Over the following days and weeks, a close bond developed and soon they were inseparable.

It was only a few months later, when Renate was told her secondment in Portugal was coming to an end, that the closeness of their relationship struck home. Renate had never thought of owning a dog, and she still didn't consider this one belonged to her in any way. At the same time, the thought of going home to Scotland was suddenly not as exciting as it should have been. Now she felt as if she was leaving something behind.

Renate found it very, very hard to say goodbye to Def, particularly as her neighbours had been talking about letting him loose once more. Renate had been involved in the debate and argued that letting him back into the wild might be a bad thing. She wasn't sure he would survive and said, "Look what happened to him last time he was out there on his own." But as she headed back to Scotland, she knew there was nothing she could do about it. It was out of her hands. Def was never far from her mind, however. Back in Aberdeen, she rang her friends in Portugal on an almost daily basis to check on Def's fate.

But events were soon conspiring to divert her thoughts in a different direction. Renate's success in her career had come at a price to her personal life. With her job requiring her to be constantly on the move, she had never settled down into a long-term relationship. But soon after she returned to Scotland, she met Barry, a man of a similar age who — like her — had been too wrapped up in his career to find time for a relationship. They clicked immediately and were soon seeing each other seriously enough to talk about a longer-term commitment.

Once more, however, Renate's work got in the way. She was called back to Portugal again. The regret she felt at leaving Barry back in Scotland was tempered by the excitement she felt at seeing Def again. On the telephone she'd heard that he was still at the residence. But her friends told her he hadn't been the same since she'd left.

She had been away for six months by the time she returned. But no sooner had she appeared in the residence quadrangle than Def was running towards her, going absolutely crazy. Renate just burst into tears and cried her eyes out. It was as if she had never been away. The two of them picked up where they had left off and were inseparable again.

Renate remained in close touch with Barry back in Scotland. They knew they had something serious and he had promised to visit her out there during her latest stay. When he came out for the first time, he met the dog about whom his girlfriend had talked so much. She had been terrified that "the two men in her life", as she called them, would not get on. Def was wary of the stranger who seemed so intimate with Renate, but the two got on perfectly well.

Barry continued popping back and forth over the following months. As their feelings for each other grew stronger rather than weaker, it became clear to them both that this was serious. Eventually, the inevitable happened and Barry summoned up the strength to propose to Renate. She didn't say "yes" immediately. She said she wanted time to think about it. It was going to entail big changes for her. She would need to change her job to cut down on her travelling. But there was something else on her mind.

Barry and Renate were sitting out in the sunshine one day when she finally summoned the strength to pop her own question. "I'd like to adopt Def and take him back to Scotland. Would you be willing for him to live with us?" she asked nervously. It had been eating away at her for ages. To Renate this was the final, acid test of whether Barry was the right man for her. She didn't think he would object, but if he did, he wasn't the person she'd imagined him to be. But she had no cause to worry.

Barry's face broke into a smile. "I wondered how long it was going to take you to ask," he said. "He's part of the family now. We couldn't go back without taking him with us."

I met them in Scotland a few years later. As often happens, we got talking and their story came tumbling out. What so impressed me was that Renate had been so committed to Def that she had been prepared to jeopardise the biggest chance of happiness she'd had in her life rather than let him down. If Barry had said no, she would have been forced to choose Def over him.

Renate, as I've said, set new standards. She showed me a level of commitment and dedication that will be hard to match. Hers is an example, I believe, from which we can all draw something.

FLEXIBLE FRIENDS

Why great owners
keep an open mind

As a breed, dog owners are notoriously prickly about criticism. Deep down, most people believe they are good owners — and they are. But they can take deep offence when someone suggests they change or rethink even the slightest little detail of how they care for their dogs.

Yet, as I know too well myself, none of us has a monopoly on wisdom, none of us knows everything. And, just as in every other sphere of life, it is a sign of strength rather than weakness to be able to admit to making mistakes and show an open mind at times.

I am fortunate in that most of the people I work with have made that admission to themselves before I even meet them. They have found themselves having problems with their dog, admitted to themselves they've made a wrong turn, and then come to me in the hope they can get back on the right road.

Everything is relative, of course, so for some people this is not such a difficult concession to make. For some people, however, performing such a U-turn requires considerable courage and flexibility of mind. Such a person was a lady I shall call Denise, a college lecturer specialising in animal — and specifically — dog behaviour.

Denise was someone who had grown up with dogs. She'd been raised on a sheep farm surrounded by Border collies. Her lifelong love of the breed had been born there, as had her interest in training them. By building on their instinctive herding abilities, she had learned how to get the best out of them as working dogs. Her sheepdogs were so good, she used to say, they could even round up chickens.

As she grew up, however, Denise realised — like so many of her generation — that farming couldn't sustain her financially. She went off to university and studied psychology and sociology, but — in truth — she still hankered for a life close to nature. She had dogs of her own by now, and spent much of her spare time running obedience and agility classes. So, when she was offered a further education course in animal behaviourism at an agricultural college, she jumped at the chance. Within a few years, she was teaching students on a National Diploma course in Animal Management in South Wales.

I first met Denise when I was invited along to speak to students on the behaviourism course. People often ask me for my opinions on behaviourism, and I hope my answers are consistent. Nobody can have anything but respect for the work of the science's leading figures, from Pavlov to Skinner and Fisher. But there is no escaping the fact that I differ from behaviourists in two fundamental ways.

Firstly, I am not someone who is steeped in professional science. Of course, I have absorbed all sorts of ideas, and there are elements in what I do that reflect accepted principles such as positive reinforcement and wolf pack theory — a subject that is receiving a lot of serious scrutiny at the moment. But my journey of discovery has been a personal one. I arrived at my theories through a combination of first-hand observation and common sense, by working with my own and other people's dogs and by using old-fashioned trial and error. I do realise that in a way this makes me an amateur rather than a professional, but as someone rather succinctly put it: "Amateurs built the ark while professionals built the *Titanic*." (And, fortunately, I've never encountered a dog who asked to see a list of my qualifications!) By working outside the conventional establishment, I believe I have developed ideas that, at the least, challenge the accepted wisdom.

The second — and, to me, most crucial — difference between myself and behaviourists is that I have always judged my method on whether it gets results, not on its scientific merit, and on whether the results are achieved in a non-violent way. Sadly, many trainers who work under the "behaviourist" banner still see force as an intrinsic part of their work. Violence or aggression of any kind is anathema to me, and always will be.

So, if I'm honest, I was expecting a rough ride in South Wales when I went into the lion's den, as it were, and spoke to a lecture hall full of behaviourism students and lecturers. I hadn't prepared anything in particular but was pleased when I learned that the class I was to address was studying the importance of hierarchy in influencing animal behaviour. If there was one subject I felt even vaguely qualified to talk about, this was it!

I had barely opened my mouth before the questions started flying at me. At first, they were coming from the students and I dealt with those easily enough. But then the class's tutor, Denise, began dominating the floor, raising her hand with a query, seemingly every couple of minutes. Her questions were prefixed with comments like, "I just don't understand this . . ." As I tried to answer she sat there scratching her head, or sometimes — even more off-puttingly — shaking it.

I always try to be honest and straightforward about what I do and how I arrived at the conclusions I did, and I did so again here. I took the students through the fundamentals of my method — from the wolf pack to my own pack, from first principles to the four key steps in my bonding process. As I did so, I saw Denise's mood change. "Oh, that makes sense," she said, at one point. Rather than doubting me, I began to see her doubting herself.

She insisted on joining me for lunch afterwards. She didn't eat — she didn't have time, she was too busy bombarding me with yet more questions. As we spoke, Denise began to tell me a little bit more about herself. She lived with four dogs, a German shepherd, a crossbreed stray she referred to as her "happy accident", and two Border collies.

Denise admitted she was having problems with all four of them. The German shepherd was very strong-willed and defiant, while the collies were generally disobedient. The crossbreed was terrified of noises, particularly thunder. She told me she'd tried all sorts of solutions, including a popular behaviourist idea, playing tapes of thunder and lightning to the dog, then feeding him at the same time.

To me this seemed all wrong. "Why are you tackling the symptoms rather than the root cause?" I asked.

"What do you mean?" she asked.

"Well, the dogs are the symptoms and we are the cause," I explained. "We have given them confusing signals, convinced them they're doing a job they are patently unqualified to carry out. If we relieve them of that job then their whole view of the world will change — and their behaviour will change with it."

I enjoy a vigorous debate, and Denise certainly pushed me hard. But by the time I left, late that Friday afternoon, at least I felt I'd gained her respect. Nevertheless, I was surprised when, a couple of days later, I had a telephone call from the person at the college who'd originally invited me to speak.

"I just thought you'd like to know I got a phone call from Denise earlier on," he said. "She told me she'd started applying your method on Friday night and by this morning her dogs were totally transformed."

Since then I've spoken to Denise again. She was very generous in her thanks and, I hope, so was I in mine. Ultimately, I can ask no more of people than that they open their mind to new ideas. These may take hold, they may not — "some will fall on stony ground", as the Biblical phrase goes — but at least they have been flexible enough to consider an alternative view of the world.

What impressed me about Denise was not so much that she had succeeded with my method, but more that she'd been brave and open-minded enough to try it in the first place. Given her professional position, she had every right to dismiss my methods, but she didn't.

Denise reminded me of something I learned during my early life from people such as my cousin Doreen. Having a flexible, free-thinking owner can make the world of difference to a dog. Nowadays, this is a point I never fail to emphasise to people, particularly those starting out on the road to dog ownership. And when I do, along with Denise and Doreen, I often cite an even more telling example of this quality at work: Frances, the proprietor of a highly-respected kennels near me.

My admiration for the people who take on the selfless task of caring for other people's dogs professionally is enormous. Some of the most impressive people I have come across have been entrusted with the job of looking after dogs at sanctuaries, rescue centres or kennels. Often they show greater care and attention to dogs than their legal owners do. Perhaps because they come into contact with such a wide variety of dogs, they also tend to be open and adaptable thinkers too. This was certainly the case with Frances.

★ ★ ★

Frances has run the kennels for as long as I've known her, which must be twenty-five years by now. People entrust their dogs to her — and she rewards that trust with an exceptional level of care. The setup at the kennels is perfect, and dogs are treated as individuals.

Two stories sum up Frances' amazing open-mindedness for me. The first relates to an occasion in the late 1990s when I visited the kennels to see how they were run. I was going around with Frances and one of her main helpers, Laura.

Frances, like me, was endlessly fascinated by dogs and was always eager to show me the collection of characters she had attracted to her kennels.

"Let me show you this one," she said with a knowing smile.

At first glance there was nothing out of the ordinary about the very friendly-looking crossbred bitch sitting in one of the kennels.

"This is Daisy," said Frances. "Her owners used to have terrible problems with her."

She explained that the dog's owners had come to her after using various kennels during their annual holiday abroad.

"Every time they came back, the poor dog had lost a lot of weight," Frances said. "She pined for them so much she didn't eat or sleep properly. It was spoiling their holidays every year. They were going away and all they could do was worry about Daisy."

One of Frances' many qualities is realism. She didn't promise to do any better than the other kennels. She simply said, "Let's see what we can do."

The owners were a little apprehensive when they left Daisy behind in a strange environment once more. Frances, however, wasted no time in making her latest arrival feel very much at home. Before the owners had left, she'd quizzed them in detail about what Daisy ate at home. She was surprised to discover that none of the other kennels they had used had ever asked them.

As the dog settled in, Frances made detailed notes on Daisy's favourite food, the quantities she normally ate and her preferred eating times. She then marked this information up on the main board at the office so that all her staff were able to stick rigidly to it.

The owners had also told Frances how much Daisy loved to play. Twice daily playtimes were already part of the routine at the kennels. But Frances made sure that Daisy got all the recreation she wanted while she was there. Frances and her assistants let her run until she gave up. Frances kept a close eye on her throughout the week. There were no signs of distress at night — and, given all the playing she was doing, she was clearing her bowl clean at every mealtime.

The owners couldn't believe it when they came back from their holiday. Instead of being greeted by an anxious, underweight pet, they found Daisy playing freely with one of Frances' assistants. She was still overjoyed to see her owners, of course, and came bounding up to them for a cuddle. But there was no question she'd been having as good a time — if not even better — than her owners during her holiday with Frances. "They were flummoxed. She'd even put on a couple of pounds," Frances said. It was obvious to the owners that at last they had found a kennels that knew how to care for their dog. Their days of moving Daisy from one different kennels to another each summer were over.

It was a couple of years later that I happened to see Daisy in Frances' kennels again. She looked a picture of health, as ever. Frances' face broke into a broad smile when I reminded her of Daisy's first visit.

"They're away for two weeks this year," she said. "Their last words to me as they left for the airport were, 'Please don't let her put on too much weight this time!'"

Frances' ability to think her way round a problem demonstrated itself in another situation that arose a few years later. It also demonstrated the extra mile that she was prepared to travel simply to make people's lives with their dogs that little bit happier.

She was approached by the son of an elderly lady who was about to be admitted to a local home. The change was going to leave her little Pomeranian dog, Megan, without someone to look after it — and Frances had been recommended as the ideal solution.

"My mother's very fond of Megan and is worried about what's going to happen to her when she's in the home. She heard of your reputation and asked me to approach you about looking after her," he explained.

Frances agreed and headed off to meet his mother the following day. The dog, it turned out, was elderly too — she was almost twelve years old. She was a lovely animal and Frances could understand how the elderly lady had become so attached to her.

As Frances talked to the mother, she made a suggestion.

"It's going to be very hard for you adapting to life in a new environment. Why don't I take Megan to see you every now and again," she suggested. This went down very well with the lady. "Would you mind? That would be wonderful," she said.

Soon afterwards the son delivered the dog to Frances. Once it had settled into life at the kennels, Frances decided to take her to see her owner at the home. It was a saddening sight. The lady's illness hadn't been apparent when Frances had first met her. But now it was clear she was suffering from Alzheimer's.

When Frances arrived with her dog, she became upset. "You're the woman who stole my Megan," she said.

Frances remained calm and reassuring. "No, I'm the lady who's looking after her for you. Remember, I came to see you."

Frances had planned to visit once a fortnight. But given the lady's memory problems, she decided this was too infrequent. Instead, she started calling in every week.

This worked much better. The lady had her good days and her bad days, but generally she recognised both Frances and the dog.

Frances had got to know the dog by now and sensed that she missed the constant company she had enjoyed, living with her owner. As it happened, Frances' own mother lived in a property adjoining the kennels where she had a little Pekinese. Frances sensed that the two would be good company for each other. But she wanted to check with Megan's owner first.

The elderly lady's reaction was one of horror. She didn't really understand what Frances was suggesting and got upset once more.

"No, she's got to stay with you. I trusted you to take care of her."

Frances reassured her and promised she wouldn't take her away from the kennels. At the same time, though, she saw that Megan was deteriorating. Her spirit seemed to be sapped by the kennels.

One day she called to see her mother. There was a gate linking the kennels to her mother's property. Ordinarily, Frances would have taken great care to make sure it was closed behind her. Today, however, she left it ajar. She also made sure that the only dog roaming free was Megan.

Within half an hour or so Megan was playing with her mother's Pekinese. The two got on like a house on fire — as did Megan with Frances' mother. The visits were repeated and the effect these had on the dog was dramatic. Her spirits improved markedly and she was soon putting on weight and generally looking a lot fitter.

The lady's son noticed this when he popped in one evening. Frances wasn't going to keep anything from him and explained what she was doing. She also explained what his mother had said.

The son understood completely. "We'll keep it our little secret, shall we?" he said with a smile.

Far from being a short-term thing, Megan has remained with Frances for four years. She was still there the last time I visited, aged sixteen, playing with her mother's Pekinese and the picture of health. The weekly visits to Megan's owner continued too.

As far as I am concerned, the importance of being flexible and open to ideas cannot be overestimated. In my experience, those owners with closed minds and dogmatic opinions are invariably those who are most resistant to — and least successful in — implementing my method. For whatever reason, they are too rigid in their thinking or, perhaps, too cautious in their attitude to take a leap of faith and approach things from a dog's perspective rather than that of a human. In contrast, people like Denise who are willing to put aside even the most strongly held views and try an alternative are inevitably the owners who get the most dramatic results.

It is one of the most powerful tools available to any owner. It is also something I use myself all the time. As I travel, helping people with their problematic pets, I am constantly faced with what seem like intractable problems, only to discover that — by thinking laterally and opening the door to previously untested possibilities — they aren't actually problems at all. The day I cease to keep an open mind will be the day I cease learning. And I don't intend that day to arrive for a while yet!

WHEN THE GOING GETS TOUGH

Why it pays to show courage under fire

We have all encountered owners who are not up to the mark, people whose relationship with their dog makes us shake our heads in despair. There are far too many of them. Just as there are qualities that distinguish great owners, there are common denominators among these bad owners too. Naiveté, laziness and ignorance are some of the most obvious failings. But, to me, their greatest weakness is cowardice. Too many people allow themselves to be beaten by circumstances, the opinions of others or — most common of all — a simple fear of failure. More often than not they simply lack the courage to be the owner that their dogs deserve.

I had always sensed that great owners are blessed with bravery. But it wasn't until I met a lady called Angela and her troubled rescue dog Timmy that I understood quite how courageous some people can be, even under the most intense fire.

★　★　★

Angela lived in a rural village in Lincolnshire. She was a housewife and a mother to three growing sons, aged between nine and fourteen. She was a great dog lover and had thought long and hard about getting one, but had wisely waited until the time was right for her, when the boys were older and she had more time to devote to the dog. Whereas her husband had had dogs before, Angela hadn't. She researched the subject thoroughly and eventually decided to take a dog from a local rescue centre.

Her choice of dog was a courageous one to begin with. The little eighteen-month-old Jack Russell was called Timmy and had arrived at the centre from the home of an elderly lady with whom he had lived since he was six months old. The lady had been in poor health and pretty much immobile, so the life Timmy had led had been an isolated and limited one. The lack of exercise, play and general attention had produced predictable results — the rescue centre describing him as "very neurotic".

Angela wasn't daunted, however. Walking around the kennels at the rescue centre she'd been drawn to Timmy. She had seen something in his nature that appealed to her. Somehow, to her he seemed loving and affectionate. Also, like so many people who take on rescue dogs, she was filled with a mild sense of mission. She knew Timmy had had a hard time of it recently and was determined to improve his life.

We live in a world filled with "dog experts". Everyone, it seems, has a view on every aspect of dog ownership. No sooner had Angela taken Timmy home than she was being bombarded by opinions. Friends, family — and even complete strangers — volunteered their views, most of which were based on the well-known "fact" that Jack Russells are "nasty", "snappy" or "aggressive".

"You'll have your work cut out with that one," went the familiar refrain.

In some ways, it is easy to work out why Jack Russells have picked up this reputation. For a start, they are a hugely popular dog, and in numerical terms one of the most common breeds in the UK. By the law of averages, they are going to be involved in more incidents than, say, an Alaskan malamute, a breed which is so rare you could probably count the number in this country in tens rather than tens of thousands. More importantly, they are also small dogs and small dogs are more likely to retaliate because people tend to see them as dogs that can be easily pushed and shoved around. The fact that they sometimes snap when people place their arms around them without warning is understandable. They are quite rightly terrified of what is about to be done to them and they respond accordingly.

Fortunately, it was here that Angela demonstrated her first small act of courage by ignoring this bad reputation. Rather than heeding any of this so-called "expert advice", she decided to trust the evidence of her own eyes instead. It was an admirable way of thinking. Unfortunately, it only marked the beginning of Angela's trials.

The change in environment proved difficult for Timmy. He struggled to settle in and within a week of arriving he was snarling and acting aggressively towards visitors. Angela felt this was a problem, but not an insurmountable one. Far worse was Timmy's reactions to her boys. He barked and ran around excitedly in their presence. When they came home from school, he rushed to bite the boys' legs as they walked up the stairs. The boys quickly became agitated and anxious around Timmy, as if he was a threat to them rather than a friend. This disappointed and worried Angela enormously, as did the discovery that Timmy's aggression could be directed towards her too.

Angela arrived in the living room one evening to find Timmy sitting on the sofa. Without thinking, she placed her arm behind Timmy gesturing for him to move. To her horror, Timmy nipped at her finger, drawing blood.

For those whose minds had been made up before the dog had even arrived, these early incidents were confirmations of the obvious — he was a bad dog and Angela had been a fool for believing otherwise. Even her husband was part of the unsympathetic majority. "Everybody told you this is what to expect," he said.

Angela's troubles brought the "experts" out in force. Soon her friends and family were queuing up to offer advice. Some said Timmy had to be locked up in a pen to protect the family. Others suggested a muzzle. Some said he had to go back to the rescue centre. There were plenty, too, who thought he should simply be put down immediately.

Yet Angela saw something in Timmy that no one else was capable of seeing. To her he was the most loving creature. She had never heard a dog purr in the way Timmy did when he nuzzled up to her. She couldn't get over how schizophrenic he was in this sense. One minute he was aggressive, the next minute he was affectionate. It didn't make sense to her — but that wasn't a reason for getting rid of Timmy.

Angela was a quiet, shy lady, unused to confrontation. Yet suddenly she found herself defending her dog with a passion that surprised even her. Her mother and her sister were among the most vocal critics of Timmy. Ordinarily, Angela let their opinions wash over her, but in this instance she fought back. "He's a good dog, you'll see," she told them repeatedly.

But the evidence for this was thin on the ground. Two months after Timmy's arrival, Angela reached the low point. One of her sons had found Timmy on his bed and gone to move him off the duvet. The bite Timmy had delivered the boy had left him screaming in pain. Timmy had sunk his teeth into the soft flesh beneath his thumb drawing blood and leaving a nasty open wound. Angela and her husband had to take him to hospital to have stitches.

Most of her family had turned against Timmy already. Angela's mother and her sister had continued their complaints and warned her that the situation was only going to get worse. In fact, in the wake of this incident, it was her mother-in-law who delivered the most damning attack. Angela was a devoted mother. She was proud of the way she had brought up her three boys. "Call yourself a good mother?" her mother-in-law accused her. "No decent mother would put her dog before her sons."

The attack left Angela reeling. For the first time since she'd taken him in, she considered taking Timmy back to the rescue centre and called them to explore the possibility. The centre knew Timmy's background and were frank: she was told that if Timmy went back to them, the likelihood was that he would be put down. She couldn't let that happen.

Her husband remained obstinate in his lack of support. "Either you sort him out or he goes," he said unequivocally.

Angela felt totally alone in the world, but it was in this, her darkest hour that her courage shone through. She spoke to the rescue centre once more, this time asking for advice on finding a trainer who might be able to help Timmy mend his errant ways. They referred her to me, and I'll never forget Angela's words when she telephoned me one evening at home. "You're Timmy's last hope," she said, close to tears.

The courage she had displayed already was obvious as soon as I went to visit her. Even during my visit to her home, I sensed how much opposition she had faced. "They all make me so mad," she said of Timmy's critics. "The more they have a go at him, the more I think I'm the only one he's got to stand up for him and I'm not going to let him down." Unfortunately, I knew her one-woman crusade was about to become even more of an uphill struggle — for a while at least.

For my method to work properly, it is vital that the whole family is involved in its implementation. If this doesn't happen, the dog receives conflicting signals and the job of removing it from leadership becomes more difficult. Angela left me in no doubt that she was not going to be working in concert with her family. Effectively, her husband and sons had given up on Timmy. They had decided it was Angela's responsibility to "cure" him of his problems — and they wanted nothing to do with the messy practicalities that went with it.

Angela had displayed a lot of courage even before this point. But, to me, the way she refused to be daunted or deflected by her family's attitude was even more admirable. Over the following days she stuck to my method diligently, working hard at getting the key message across to Timmy that she was in charge of the home, not him. Her perseverance produced almost immediate results. Within days, Timmy was coming to her when she asked him and behaved in a much calmer, less confrontational way around her. Of course, her friends and family were dismissive — often downright rude — about her unusual new training method. Fortunately, she could soon draw solace from the results she achieved.

It was one evening, about three weeks after I'd visited her, that the turning point came. Angela was alone with her husband and Timmy. Timmy was playing affectionately with Angela and her husband made a move towards him, putting his arms out, as if to join in the fun — but was rewarded with a bite to his stockinged foot.

"How come he does that to me and not to you?" he asked, exasperated.

Angela smiled at him and said: "Well, I could tell you, if you like."

Angela explained that, as far as Timmy was concerned, she was above him within the domestic hierarchy. Her husband, however, was not.

"It was his way of telling you that you aren't entitled to approach him like that. You were invading his space and he hadn't invited you to do so," she told him. "He doesn't do that to me because I've earned the right to tell him what to do as leader. He accepts that I have the right to invade his body space."

Angela was delighted to see her husband sitting there nodding quietly.

"I get it," he said at the end. "So how do I become a leader as well?"

That night Angela's husband began implementing the method. The results could not have been more dramatic. Within two days, Timmy was behaving as well with him as he did with Angela.

That weekend, the family were sitting in the living room watching television together. Timmy had been playing nicely with Angela and her husband but when one of the boys tried to ruffle his head, he received a snap and a growl.

"It's your own fault," their father told them, much to Angela's delight.

"If you bothered to learn how to behave with the dog, he wouldn't be snapping at you." Angela was over the moon to hear this. As the boys began to behave in the same way as their parents, she finally began to see the light at the end of the tunnel.

Soon the atmosphere in the house was totally transformed. Instead of a growling, snarling puppy, visitors were greeted by the sight of a fun, affectionate dog. When Angela received a visit from a relative from overseas, he was deeply impressed and came out with the priceless line: "He's not like a normal Jack Russell, is he?"

During the first crucial weeks following my visit, I'd stayed in close contact with Angela. But as things calmed down, however, we'd spoken less and less. It was almost a year later before I heard from her again.

"Remember me?" she said.

"Of course I do, how's Timmy?" I replied.

"Great, never been better," she said.

We chatted for a while, Angela enthusing about the active life Timmy was now enjoying with her and the boys. But she had called me for a specific reason and soon got to the point.

"The reason I'm ringing is that I'm getting another Jack Russell from the rescue centre, a girl this time," she said. "I was wondering if you had any advice on introducing them to each other."

I was simply bowled over by Angela's sheer guts. It hadn't been so long ago that she had been driven to the depths of despair by the challenge of taking on a rescue dog — yet now here she was ready to go through the same thing again.

If it had been a different owner, I might have counselled her against it. But this was someone who'd already shown all the qualities of an outstanding owner. Needless to say, Timmy and his new pal were soon living happily under the same roof. And needless to say too, I was soon citing their remarkable owner as someone who had shone an uplifting and inspiring new light on dog ownership for me.

Courage comes in different guises. Often, as in the case of Angela, it is an ability to hang on in there, to tough it out. But it can also be the courage to take a single decision. It was this kind of courage that I saw displayed by a lady called Linda.

Linda lived with her dog, a German shepherd called Khan, in Boston, Lincolnshire. When she'd first acquired him she had — like any responsible owner — looked around for the best way to train him. Unfortunately, she'd chosen an obedience class in her area. The lady who ran the class was a type I've encountered many times. "I've been around dogs for thirty years," she boomed at Linda with a dismissive look. "The first thing you've got to do is show them who is boss." As it happens, she was right in that respect. But in every other respect, particularly in the way that she chose to impose her will on the dogs in her class, she was dreadfully — and dangerously — wrong.

Khan was not the boldest of dogs. But nor was he defiant. Yet despite this, the trainer insisted that Linda

95

use the traditional choke chain to jerk him around the hall. She felt deeply uncomfortable about this, but, as she put it to me, "This woman was the expert, not me. I didn't think I knew any better and didn't argue."

She kept returning to the class but each time she did so her misgivings deepened. Each time, the trainer was being physical with Khan, who was also clearly unhappy with this.

Things came to a head one week when the class came to teaching "the sit". Once more the method recommended by the trainer involved using force.

"If they see you are weak they will walk away from you," she told the class. She then showed how the dog should be taught to sit by being physically pushed into position.

She did this with Khan, grabbing hold of him at the base of his neck then forcing his hind legs down into the sit position. As she did so, Khan let out a bloodcurdling yelp.

"Could you do it a bit gentler?" Linda asked the lady.

"I'm being cruel to be kind," the trainer said. "Don't you worry. I've been working with dogs for thirty years. You'll thank me for it in the end." By now Linda's doubts were massing in her mind. The second time the trainer pushed Khan down he yelped again, this time even louder. "Oh, he's a male, dear, they're all wimps," the trainer bellowed.

Linda went home that night deeply distressed. "I can't keep putting him through this, it's hell for him," she told her husband Tony. "I just don't see that this is the way to work with a dog. There has to be a better way."

Linda went with her feelings and stayed away from the class from that night onwards. She hadn't learned to control Khan as well as she would have wanted, and she had her fair share of problems with him. But to her it was far preferable to having him physically assaulted by this so-called expert. She was determined to keep trying other approaches in the hope that — somewhere — there was one that did not involve such distress.

A short time after she left the classes, Khan needed to go to the vet for a routine course of injections. The vet wasn't particularly happy with Khan and performed a thorough examination, including an X-ray. Afterwards he took Linda to one side and said, "I'm afraid I've got some bad news."

He told her that Khan had a chronic case of hip displacia, a common and very painful hereditary problem in German shepherds. But in Khan's case it was so severe it severely limited his mobility.

"It means he's not going to be very comfortable, and you are going to have to restrict the amount of exercise he can do," he said. "It will also help if you keep him calm and stress-free so that he doesn't put too much strain on himself."

Linda just burst into tears.

"Don't worry, it's not life-threatening. You'll still be able to lead a full life together," the vet consoled her, assuming — quite understandably — that she was crying at the diagnosis he'd just given.

"Oh, it's not that, I know we'll be fine," Linda said, still sobbing. "It's the fact that I let that bloody dog trainer bully him."

Linda was so angry at herself for not having trusted in her feelings sooner. She felt ashamed for not intervening earlier and stopping the trainer push Khan around. "Why didn't I listen to my instincts?" she said. "I knew it was wrong, and I was too weak to do anything about it. Poor dog."

I got to know her soon after she made this discovery. By implementing my method she improved Khan's behaviour hugely. Most importantly, she got him to relax a lot more, which in turn eased the strain on his legs and hips and reduced the discomfort the displacia gave him.

Talking to her about her experience, Linda reminded me so much of myself years earlier. It had been at an obedience class that I too had first felt misgivings about the traditional, confrontational training methods. I had seen women like the one who had hurt Khan inflict distress on my own dogs. Those same nagging doubts had assailed me, and — like Linda — I regretted every day the fact that I had not acted on my instincts earlier.

"I just wish I'd been braver and listened to my instincts sooner," she said.

"Well, at least you did listen and were brave enough to do something before it was too late," I replied. "If only that were true of all owners."

There is a lesson there for us all, I believe.

THE GREAT HEALER

Why patience really is a virtue

My maternal grandmother used to have a saying: "If you run into a room you'll hit your head on something." By this she meant, if you charge at something you'll get nowhere, whereas if you weigh something up in advance you're more likely to succeed.

She instinctively understood something that has become absolutely central to the work I do: patience really is a virtue.

We live in a world of instant gratification. People seem to want everything not just now, but yesterday. There is an obsession with the quick fix, the miracle on demand. Some owners seem unwilling — or even unable — to appreciate that some things aren't solved in a minute, a day or even a week. The word patience doesn't seem to exist in their dictionaries.

If anyone taught me the value and true meaning of patience, it was Ruth, a kennel maid I met back in the 1980s.

At the time, I was heavily involved with an animal sanctuary near my home in Barnetby, Lincolnshire. It had been my job as a part-time newspaper columnist, writing about animal matters, that had taken me there. At first I'd been shocked by the cruelty previously inflicted on the animals entrusted to the centre's care. Some of the cats, dogs and horses that had been handed in were in a terrible state.

As I'd got to know the sanctuary's charismatic owner, Miss D, and her staff, I'd been hugely impressed by the compassion and dedication involved in putting these poor creatures back together again. One thing led to another and before I knew it I'd begun helping out when I had spare time, first running a small dog show then giving a hand with general duties from mucking out and walking the dogs to helping with feeding.

I got immense satisfaction from it and I felt I was making a small difference to their lives. In terms of dedication and sheer patience, however, I was not in the same class as the sanctuary's head maid, Ruth.

It had been Miss D who had first told me about her remarkable work. One day, while passing the bungalow where Ruth lived on the edge of the sanctuary, I noticed she had two dogs, one a Cocker spaniel, called Luke, and a good-looking greyhound called Dudley. I knew that Miss D's strict rules meant that no staff member was allowed two dogs. When I asked her about Ruth's pair she'd explained that she'd turned a blind eye because of the extraordinary job she had done with Dudley.

"Dudley?" I'd asked, slightly surprised.

When I'd seen him earlier that day he'd looked a fine example of the breed. His muscle condition was excellent, his coat shone. He looked as if he could run in the greyhound Derby — and win.

"He's all right now," Miss D said, shaking her head solemnly. "But if you'd seen that dog when he arrived here, and if you knew what that girl did to make him better."

It was only when I got to know Ruth in the coming weeks and months that I understood what she meant. Ruth was a quiet girl, so the story came out in a slow, understated way. But it didn't make it any less inspiring.

Greyhounds aren't always treated well when their racing days are over. There are some owners who place their dogs in good homes, but there are a large number for whom greyhounds are nothing more than a moneymaking entertainment. When their racing days are over, they are mistreated, abandoned — or even worse. It is an attitude selfish beyond belief, and it is also a mindset that is far too prevalent.

Dudley was one of the unlucky ones. He had been found a year or so earlier in a truly dreadful state. It was clear he was a former racing greyhound because he still had the telltale registration number inside his ear. But he was a pale shadow of the athletic creature that people had paid money to see racing.

As Ruth related the story, I realised I had known about Dudley even before meeting him, or getting to know Miss D and the sanctuary. The newspaper I worked on, the *Lincolnshire Times*, had run a piece on an abandoned greyhound. Stories about discarded and abused dogs were standard fare for a country newspaper like ours, but even allowing for that, his story — together with his picture — was shocking. It was little wonder I hadn't associated that pathetic creature with the healthy animal in Ruth's garden.

The Dudley I remembered from the photograph was an appalling sight. There is something heart-wrenching about a sickly greyhound because, even when they are in top condition, they are naturally thin. Ruth told me that Dudley was so thin you could reach around his waist with your hand. He was also absolutely covered in fleas. When Ruth took him to a vet he was diagnosed with sarcoptic mange, the worst and most highly contagious strain of the parasite.

Ruth had cared for many dogs at the sanctuary, but she'd rarely seen one in such a state. "He was a broken dog," she told me. "I had to try and put him back together again."

The first thing she had to do was to tackle the mange. It is a terrible condition that drives a dog to despair — scratching itself incessantly and becoming aggressive when the itching doesn't go away. It can drag a dog down fast. Ruth put Dudley in isolation in the sanctuary's hospital, where she treated him with the prescribed drugs, at the same time beginning the long, slow process of feeding him back up. Dudley was so weak and poorly he wanted to sleep all the time. However, this was a luxury Ruth was willing to forgo. For the first few weeks she got up three times each night to walk from her bungalow over to the hospital. There she administered the injections and carefully fed Dudley some scrambled eggs or chopped chicken.

Slowly the mealtimes were spread out to every three hours, then every four.

As Ruth told me about the work she'd done, two things began to become clear. The first was that she had the patience of the proverbial saint. If necessary, she would have taken a decade to bring Dudley back to health, that was obvious. Even more significant was the disciplined, businesslike way she went about treating Dudley. Ruth felt strongly about Dudley, of course, but she understood she had a job to do, and that job consisted of series of priorities — the first of which was putting Dudley on the road to physical recovery. "I didn't make a big fuss over him at first," she told me. "It was much more important that I just concentrated on getting him well."

Progress was painfully slow. To begin with, Dudley showed few signs of regaining strength, and he seemed to sleep every hour God sent. Eventually, after a few weeks, Ruth managed to build him up sufficiently to get him to take a few short steps outside his kennel. It wasn't an epic walk by any stretch of the imagination, but it felt like he was making progress at last.

After three months or so, the mange had disappeared and Dudley had recovered some of his strength. Ruth explained that having restored Dudley physically, she then began the job of restoring him emotionally and psychologically. Of course, this process had really started in the hospital. Dudley had grown to trust Ruth in a way he had not been able to trust a human before. But there still had been little real affection between the two. With phase one over, it was now time for them to

103

bond in this way, and Ruth took him back to her bungalow on the sanctuary grounds.

This was never going to be easy given the nervousness Dudley was still displaying. There was also the matter of her other dog Luke, a lively creature who immediately set Dudley on edge.

Dudley was an abused dog, and despite the good work Ruth had done, he remained a bundle of nerves for the first few days. Again, Ruth knew the worst thing she could do was rush the process. So she did all she could to keep him and Luke apart. While Luke spent a lot of time outside, Dudley remained in a room she had prepared especially for him.

For a long time he reacted badly to visitors. While occasionally he would walk a little around Ruth's garden, he remained weak. The long process of building up his strength still had some way to go.

I knew there were plenty of willing hands at the sanctuary, so at one point I wondered why Ruth hadn't enlisted someone else's help. "Couldn't someone have shared the burden with you?" I asked her.

"It took me ages to get him to trust me. Someone had done something so terrible that he found it really hard to put his faith in a human again," she said. "I needed him to know he was safe and I couldn't risk someone else endangering that."

Ruth continued working with every other dog in the sanctuary as well. But for more than a year she was the only one who worked with Dudley.

Her dedication had eventually borne fruit. Day by day, week by week and month by month, Dudley had regained both his strength and his trust in humans. About eighteen months after he first arrived, Ruth was able to walk him around the sanctuary and the local countryside without him flinching or reacting in any way. He was a broken dog no longer.

Each time she talked about Dudley, I listened to Ruth's story, rapt with admiration. The most telling moment came when I told her how strong my admiration was.

We were out walking a couple of dogs one morning. She'd told me a little more about her work with Dudley. "Gosh, you're something special to devote that much of your time and energy to a dog like that," I remember telling her.

She immediately shot me a quizzical, almost dismissive look.

"How could I not do it?" she said. "Anyone would have done the same."

Even then, I knew how wrong she was there.

"If only that were true, Ruth," I told her.

A couple of years later Ruth was offered a job at a bigger boarding kennels in the area. To absolutely no one's surprise she took Dudley — and Luke — with her.

Even back then, Ruth exemplified many of the qualities that make a great dog owner. In bringing Dudley back to life, she showed a selflessness and devotion that was way above and beyond the call of duty. Most impressive of all, however, she'd shown a level of patience and a sense of priority that was remarkable. As I began to work with dogs more widely myself, her example only grew in importance.

From the outset, many of the dogs I was asked to help were rescue dogs. None, thankfully, was in as terrible a state as Dudley, but they were "broken" in their own way nevertheless. Owners tended to react in almost exactly the same way to the arrival of a rescue dog. They wanted to cuddle and care for them, smother them with love, as if to compensate for the deprivations of the past. This, from the beginning, left me with a harsh lesson to deliver.

Giving them affection is perfectly natural, but it is not the priority. Their first job is to heal the dogs, give them any medication they need, and also make them feel safe and secure within a pack environment that they understand. To do this according to my method by establishing leadership requires a degree of disengagement — a degree of formality — that people often find hard to accept. There is affection, of course, but as I always put it, it must be affection in a different direction.

As I had found with owners such as Terry and Sandra, and their dog Guinness, getting owners to grasp and apply this is one of the hardest things I am asked to do. The more severe the damage a dog has suffered in its previous home, and the more troubled or lost it seems, the more people want to love it. Yet the fact is they should, in general terms, be doing the opposite. This is where Ruth's story has always proved so invaluable.

Being able to tell people about the work Ruth did with Dudley — and explaining how she'd slowly and methodically approached the job, in particular — has helped me enormously over the years. And for that I owe her a huge debt of gratitude.

A DOG IS FOR LIFE

Why great owners understand the meaning of responsibility

It's the oldest of clichés, but true nevertheless: a dog isn't just for Christmas, it's for life.

Dog ownership brings with it a set of very real responsibilities — it is not something to be taken lightly. Yet the depressing truth is that far too many owners give up on their dogs at the first sign of trouble, unable — or unwilling — to meet their responsibilities. Animal sanctuaries and dogs' homes are filled with the victims of their failure.

It is no use denying that living up to this responsibility can be a tough task. At times, it can seem impossible. During the course of my work, I have seen intelligent, loving and deeply committed owners crack under the strain of trying to cope with their dogs' seemingly uncontrollable behaviour.

Yet I have also seen how the very best owners seem to be equipped with an ability not only to meet the challenges they face, but also to grow stronger as the scale of those problems grow. Somehow, these people are capable of living up to the responsibility in a way

108

that surprises even them. I have met a few outstanding examples of this over the years, but none was more impressive — or instructive — than a lady called Michelle.

Michelle lived with her husband John and their three children in a lovely three-bedroom house with a huge garden in Barnsley. Their children had been pestering them about having a dog for years, but it was only as they reached a more mature age, at the end of primary school, that Michelle and John finally relented. All five of them were delighted to welcome George, a lively bull mastiff puppy, into the home.

Everyone knows that bull mastiffs are very powerful dogs. They are also perceived as aggressive and troublesome dogs. What few people seem to understand is that the bull mastiff is a highly intelligent dog, which is why it has a habit of getting into so much trouble. George was no exception. He knew he could intimidate because he saw the way people backed off when he barked. So, as he settled into family life, he would stand with his shoulders square, using his piercing round eyes to full effect.

When she committed to having George, Michelle made another commitment. She was determined to fulfil her responsibilities to him — no matter what. George was soon testing that promise to the limit. As he grew from a puppy into a young dog and settled into life with Michelle and John, his aggression intensified.

He was aggressive towards visitors and was vocal, barking all the time. Even taking him for a walk down

109

the road was a problem. George pulled so hard Michelle was left hanging on with both hands for dear life. At times, it was more like skiing than walking. It didn't faze her, however. From the outset, Michelle's view had been that a dog is for life, not just some whim.

When they had questioned George's behaviour, Michelle and John had been told that this was what a mastiff did. They either lived with him or had him put down. Their reaction was admirable. "Well, we'll live with him," they said. They did this even though they knew it was going to involve a change in their lifestyle. If that was what was required, then so be it. They were prepared to take on the responsibility — and they managed it well.

For outsiders this was a hard thing to understand. To them George was nothing but a problem. As often happens, friends and family began staying away from the house because of George.

But living with George was a different matter. When the five of them were together as a family, he was fine. To John, Michelle and the children he was the perfect dog, a great loving companion. There were the odd drawbacks, most notably that they couldn't have a cuddle on the sofa. If they did, George immediately began barking and prising them apart by jamming his head between them. They were even prepared to make that compromise. If they wanted a cuddle, they reasoned, they could do it in another room, away from George. At the root of their thinking was an acceptance that, however difficult he made their lives, George's

110

behavioural problems were not of his own making. "It's not his fault," Michelle would say.

Things grew progressively more serious, however. At one point their neighbours complained about George's incessant barking in the garden. Michelle and John were visited by the local authorities, who issued them with a warning. Their greatest fear, however, was that George would attack someone. "If he bites someone, that's it. He'll be put down," Michelle would say. They began to live in constant fear.

It was here that they went to the most extraordinary lengths. Michelle, John and the family enjoyed taking camping holidays. When it came to their first trip away with George, they were so concerned about him attacking someone else that John decided to sleep with the dog. He actually tied himself to George in the kitchen area of the tent.

"He only pulled him out of the tent while he was sleeping the once," Michelle said afterwards — as if this was some kind of achievement. "To be honest, Jan, it wasn't a holiday. It was an endurance test," she added with a sigh.

By the time George had been with Michelle and John for three years, their lives had been transformed into something approaching purgatory. Even the most supportive of their friends and family no longer came to visit them. On the rare occasions they did speak with them, their nearest and dearest would tell them that George would have to go. It was a classic case of "give a dog a bad name". Bull mastiffs had a poor reputation and now this had become something of a self-fulfilling prophecy.

After a while they were being told that many owners of bull mastiffs had them put down between the ages of three and four. "You won't be able to handle him any more," Michelle was told. "He'll have too much power for you." Yet Michelle and John refused to contemplate this. They remained as devoted and loyal to George as they knew he was to them.

Some find it hard to understand why people can be so devoted to a dog, but to owners like Michelle the loyalty is instinctive. She admitted that she saw George in the same way she saw her children. We all want other people to love our children the way we love them, and it is distressing when people don't warm to them because of their misbehaviour — or even worse make clear their dislike.

But none of us would think of giving up our children just because they failed to generate the same devotion in others. "That's the way I see it with George," Michelle would say. "You wouldn't expect me to give up one of my children, and you can't expect me to give up on my dog."

Fortunately, she didn't need to give up on him.

I came across the family as part of the television series *The Dog Listener*, in which I was asked to help dogs with severe behavioural problems. When my co-presenter Paul Hendy went along to see George he was horrified. "He was ready to bite my head off," he told me. But as soon as I met Michelle I knew she was an exceptional owner.

She was a straight-talking woman. She would call a spade a shovel. But she was also a kind person — and she was adamant that she wasn't going to let this dog down. I found that hugely admirable, and sensed that she would be as good as her word. Sure enough, within three weeks of adopting my method, George had been transformed.

When Paul returned with the cameras, he couldn't believe the contrast. Paul was able to call George to him. And when he asked him for his paw, George extended it without a moment's hesitation, dropping it into his new friend's extended palm with a loud "boomph".

I had seen people face up to formidable odds over the years — I remembered Angela and her Jack Russell Timmy, for instance — but this was a different kind of problem. For a start, Timmy, for all his energy and occasional snappiness, had never posed a serious risk to people. He was a small dog, and as such he represented a relatively small threat. George was an entirely different matter. The damage he could cause didn't bear thinking about. Michelle had a really rough time, but she never once thought of letting George down. In the end, thanks to perseverance and a host of other admirable qualities, she found a way through. And because she got George when a puppy, the transformation in his behaviour was all the more dramatic. Again, the comparison with Timmy is a good one. As a rescue dog, Timmy had carried a lot more emotional and psychological baggage. It had taken his owner longer to achieve a transformation that, in real terms, was not as great as that George had demonstrated.

I remember admiring the resolve Michelle had shown and I recall feeling delighted for her now that George was a totally changed dog. They'd always enjoyed each other's company, but with the new, relaxed atmosphere at home, the family were revelling in their dog's company more than ever.

They had all been there for George during the bad times. As I left them, I felt sure they were all going to enjoy the good times. I felt sure too that one day I would use them as an example to others, which is why I have included them here.

99% PREPARATION

Why great owners think ahead

You can tell that some people are going to be great owners before they've even acquired a dog. Sometimes they have an air of calm and competence about them. Sometimes they exude a passion for dogs that you just know will overcome all obstacles. Sometimes it is simply the way dogs behave in their company. But, in my experience, one of the strongest signs of a natural dog owner is the degree of planning they are willing to put in ahead of a dog joining their home.

Everyone can get inspired by the idea of having a dog, it's the easiest thing in the world to go "aaah" at an angelic-looking puppy and imagine a life of blissful happiness. But the reality is that having a dog means a lot of work — much of it before the dog has even arrived in the home.

It wasn't until I met a lady called Lily that I realised quite how important a factor this can be.

Lily was well into her sixties and had been a passionate dog person all her life. She was a particular fan of poodles, and in recent years had begun providing a home for rescued members of that breed.

She was going through a rare dogless period when she was called by her local rescue centre about a new arrival: a poodle called Benji. It was unclear why Benji had been given to the centre, but somehow a previous owner had been able to give them quite detailed information about him. Benji was eight years old and was described as "neurotic". By this they meant he jumped up a lot, got very excited at times and barked almost incessantly.

The most worrying aspect of his personality, however, was his inability to deal with loud bangs, and fireworks in particular. The rescue centre had learned that during the run-up to the previous Bonfire Night, Benji had become so distressed that he had had to be heavily sedated by a local vet on November 5th.

I learned all this from Lily when — completely out of the blue — she rang me one evening, shortly after she'd been asked to take Benji into her care. She told me she was considering taking on Benji, but before she committed herself she wanted some advice in advance, specifically about dealing with his fear of loud bangs.

"I've heard that you can do special things with dogs, so I was wondering whether there was any way you could help a dog with this problem," she said.

I immediately liked Lily for several reasons. First of all, anyone who was willing to put themselves out as she did on behalf of poorly treated dogs had my admiration. I could also tell she was a real character, a spirited personality, a woman of strong opinions and will — someone I could relate to.

116

But more than anything, I really liked her approach. My telephone rings constantly from around the end of October until the first few days of November. I am inundated with calls from people whose dogs have begun reacting to the start of the firework season and are desperate for a solution in time for Bonfire Night on November 5th. In most cases, they're cutting it very fine and have often left it too late to see a marked change in their dog's behaviour.

What impressed me about Lily was her foresight. She was not only tackling this six months early — in May — she was also addressing the problem before even agreeing to let Benji live with her. "It would break my heart to have to see a dog go through that torture," she told me. "I don't want to give him drugs either, so if you tell me there's nothing I can do, I'll have to have a good think about whether this is a good idea at all."

As we chatted on the phone and she described Benji to me, it was obvious that she was from an older generation of dog owners. "He barks and jumps around a lot but that's only natural in a poodle," she said. I didn't respond, instead I took her through the basic principles of my method.

This had been one of the very first problems I'd encountered in my own life with dogs. As a teenager I'd spent many an anxious hour on and around Bonfire Night, consoling and comforting my first dog Shane. I had since realised that I had been given an insight into the cure during my encounter with the fairground owner I met in my local park. I knew now that it was down to leadership and conveying to the dog that there was nothing to worry about. If I had ignored the bangs and explosions, and simply thanked Shane each time he responded to them, I would have avoided all the anguish.

I explained this to Lily, emphasising that first she would have to assert herself as Benji's leader. "One thing will lead to the other," I told her. "If Benji believes in you as a leader, he will accept your word whatever you say."

As I explained this to Lily, her reaction wasn't untypical. There were a few "I'm sorry, what did you say?"s and "Are you sure?"s. "Hmmm, I think I see," she said, after a while. It was a couple of weeks before I heard from her again.

"Just thought I'd give you an update, dear," she said. She was an elderly lady but she was switched on and had realised how she must have come across during our first conversation. "I don't know what you must have thought of me but I was digesting what you had to say. You don't think it's natural for a dog to jump up and act neurotically at all, do you?" she said.

"Well, no, but I'm not going to force my opinions on everyone," I said.

"Perhaps you should, dear," she said. "Perhaps you should. I read *The Dog Listener* and was fascinated. I think you're on to something there," she said. "I'm going to go ahead and have Benji. And I'm going to treat him the way you recommend and see how we get on. I'll keep you posted, dear."

It was always a pleasure to hear from Lily. There was something admirable about her personality; she must have been a remarkable woman when she was younger. Each time she called she was making good progress. She'd used my four-step process to underline constantly her place at the head of her mini-hierarchy. Happy to be demoted to junior status within his pack, Benji's "neurotic" personality had all but disappeared. He was happy and relaxed around the home, and she'd made headway out on walks when he heard unexpected noises, such as cars backfiring or planes overhead.

"I keep telling myself not to react," Lily told me. "It's hard sometimes to ignore their distress, but I've learned now that it works."

The call I had been most anticipating came in late October, almost six months after her first enquiry. Benji had continued his good work but that week the acid test had finally presented itself. The firework season seems to start earlier and earlier these days. Lily lived on a busy estate, made up of bungalows for the elderly as well as family homes. For the past few evenings, the local youngsters had begun firing rockets and letting off bangers and the like.

Lily told me that she'd been quietly dreading the evening when the first bang went off in her street. Sure enough, when it came, Benji dived underneath the nearest piece of furniture, a sideboard. He lay there, shivering, looking in her direction.

For all the success she'd had, Lily knew this was the make-or-break moment. All her instincts were to go to Benji and console him. But now she understood that to do that would have been to confirm his instinct that there was something wrong. As his leader, Lily had to

119

convince Benji the exact opposite — that there was absolutely nothing to worry about.

It was a battle, but she managed it. "I just sat there on the sofa, reminding myself of your advice: 'Don't react.' 'Don't react.' It was really hard," she said.

It didn't get any easier when, a few moments later, there was another bang. The noise was so thunderous, Lily almost jumped herself, but again she kept her composure. "Benji kept looking at me, but I kept avoiding eye contact," she said.

For the next half hour or so there was no let-up. But after the umpteenth bang, Benji began slowly creeping out from under the side-board. Very, very gingerly he then walked towards Lily on the sofa.

As the skies outside continued to light up, Lily invited him to slip on to her lap. "He was trembling a little bit, but I kept checking my pulse and telling myself to keep it down, to stay calm," she said. He remained there, sitting quietly until the fireworks were over. Over the following evenings, the same thing had happened again. Each time, however, Benji simply shot Lily a look, then either came to her or stayed in his bed until the explosions had subsided.

The last conversation I had with Lily was a memorable one. She told me that the rescue centre had made a special point of calling round to see her during the run-up to Bonfire Night. The visitors had barely begun talking about their ideas about how to steer Benji through this year's ordeal when Lily interrupted them.

"Oh, we've cured all that," she said, dismissing it as if it were nothing.

I can just imagine the triumphant look on her face as she said it.

Lily's example was a truly admirable one. Despite her advanced years, she was willing to open her mind to new ideas, to try something different for the sake of improving a dog's life. But it was the foresight she showed in planning ahead that was most impressive.

Since my early days as an owner, I've sensed the importance of preparation in dog ownership. I've seen so many dogs arrive in households completely unprepared for their arrival. And I've seen the inevitable unhappy consequences of that lack of planning. In working with new owners or people adding new dogs to existing packs, I always stress the importance of laying the groundwork. For instance, I always advise people acquiring new puppies to spend time visiting the dog in its litter. When people incorporate new dogs into existing packs, I suggest they introduce the expanded pack to each other on "neutral ground".

Lily did more than simply confirm the correctness of this approach. She made me realise it is absolutely fundamental. She helped me see that sometimes good ownership is a matter of 1% inspiration and 99% preparation. And for that I will always be thankful to her.

THE BUCK STOPS HERE

Why great owners always shoulder the blame

Every now and again I'm asked: can I tell a good dog owner simply by looking at them? Is there something that, in just a few seconds, gives away whether or not that person has a loving and successful relationship with their dog?

Dog ownership is not like golf, say, where coaches reckon they can spot a good or bad player simply by the way they address the ball on the tee. Much of it is down to the personalities involved — both human and canine — so the question is a tricky one. But, if pressed, my answer is a conditional "yes". Show me the way a person reacts when their dog makes what they perceive to be a mistake, and I'll probably be able to tell you whether they are a good owner or not. Good owners blame themselves — bad ones blame their dogs.

To me, anyone who blames their dog for failing to understand them is heading completely down the wrong road. How can we fault a dog for failing to respond to a request that's been delivered in a language it doesn't understand? We all know dogs are highly intelligent. But do we think they are so bright they are mind-readers? Clearly it is up to us to communicate effectively with them and it can never be the other way round. And if this is the case, then it follows that if there is a communication breakdown and they are failing to do what we expect them to do, it is our fault not theirs. Yet, despite this, so many people chide their dogs for failing to listen properly to them.

We have all seen owners ranting and raving at their dogs — or even worse, hitting them — all because they've failed to obey an instruction or they have done something the owner has deemed to be wrong. Equally, we have all seen the seemingly endless patience of the owner who spends hours throwing a ball around the park, working hard to get their relationship with their dog right. In instances like this, I'm sure we could all tell which two ends of the ownership scale they represent.

During the course of my career, I've encountered plenty of people who would fail this kind of "instant owner test". By the same token, I have seen many pass it with flying colours. Few, however, did so as impressively as Maria, a trainer with the charity Dogs for the Disabled.

Dogs for the Disabled is an admirable organisation providing working pets for people with varying degrees of disability. It is quite amazing the range of jobs that their wonderfully trained dogs can carry out for their "partners" — everything from opening and closing doors and offering help across pedestrian crossings to fetching and carrying food and drinks and even dressing their disabled companions.

I have become quite actively involved with Dogs for the Disabled over the years. It was while visiting their centre at Banbury, near Oxford, that I met Maria for the first time.

As it happened, I was accompanied that day by a reporter from BBC Radio 4's popular *Woman's Hour* programme. They were doing a piece on me and my work and had wanted to record some material in an interesting environment, and the Dogs for the Disabled centre certainly fitted the bill. Dogs arrive at the purpose-built centre at around one year old and are trained to perform a range of tasks. They are then put together with their "partner", who stays at the centre until the trainers feel both dog and owner are ready for the challenges of the wider world.

As I say, the skills the dogs learn there are remarkable. They will teach them to help people both in the home and out in the community, whether out on the streets or in shops. In general terms, the dogs are taught five essential skills: the pull, the push, the target, the fetch and the speak. The pull requires them to pull open doors around the house, from dividing doors to cupboard or washing machine doors. The push is the opposite, closing doors and appliances. The target teaches the dog to use its paws to touch specific objects, such as light switches, or the buttons on pelican crossings. The fetch teaches them to retrieve objects, from remote controls to purses, keys to clothes. Finally, the speak teaches the dog to raise the alarm by barking a particular bark that will be recognisable to neighbours or carers.

The journalist was fascinated by what she saw, as anyone would have been. After Maria had explained the basic principles of the programme and training process, she asked whether it would be possible to see a dog at work.

Maria was happy to oblige and headed off to the kennelling area, soon returning accompanied by Tangle, a one-year-old yellow Labrador–Retriever cross. Dogs for the Disabled works almost exclusively with this type of breed; the Labrador's intelligence and natural ability as a retrieving gundog make it ideal to undertake the range of duties required. It is also a good-sized dog and easy to maintain — an important factor when dealing with people who have a limited ability to reach to the ground.

The reporter wanted to set up some recording equipment before the demonstration began. As she set about getting things ready, Tangle lay on the floor near Maria where he promptly fell asleep. He remained there until things were ready, when Maria woke him up.

Maria wanted to simulate something that typified the day-to-day routine a dog such as Tangle would face. Climbing into a wheelchair, she flicked up its collapsible footplates before issuing Tangle an instruction to "push". To help him along, Maria also pointed to the footplates. Rather than approaching the wheelchair, however, Tangle decided to take two steps back and pull at the toggle on the nearby door, hauling it open in one movement.

"Oh, that wasn't very good, was it?" the reporter said, approaching Maria with her microphone. Maria just smiled, looking unperturbed.

"It's fine. It's natural for dogs to do that this early in their training," she said. She was quite right, of course — for young dogs, pulling at things is the most natural thing in the world. Of the five actions that are taught, it is by far the most instinctive.

A few moments later Maria tried again. Once more, when she said push Tangle went to pull at the door.

"Why is the dog getting it wrong?" the reporter asked.

"He isn't," Maria replied calmly. "It's my mistake. Tangle has only just woken up and I should have warmed him up with a few simple pulls before we started. This isn't the ideal environment for training."

On the third attempt, Tangle pushed down the footplate just as Maria had asked him to. When he did so, he was rewarded with a ruffle of his neck and some quiet praise. "Good dog," Maria said repeatedly using positive reinforcement. "Good dog."

This time the reporter asked Maria why the dog had taken three attempts. "That's nothing to worry about at this stage. He did very well," she said. "His training is going very well and he'll make a great dog in time."

I had kept a discreet distance while Maria had been putting Tangle through his paces. But I remember standing in the wings smiling quietly to myself. "Good for you," I said to myself.

126

In a way it was a very small incident. Yet it spoke volumes about Maria and her approach to the dogs entrusted to her at the centre. Even in a professional environment like this, there would have been owners who would have blamed the dog for making the mistake.

This was a very artificial situation. Maria was completely unfamiliar with radio or television work and must have felt slightly pressurised by the presence of a microphone, recording her at work. Yet she remained completely calm with Tangle. She understood instinctively that to act embarrassed or become angry with a dog is to court disaster. Dogs will pick up on the panic or aggression and reproduce it themselves. She would have done more harm than good by doing so. Of course, the reporter was only doing her job, but it would have been easy for Maria to lose patience with her questioning. Instead, she remained calm.

But most importantly of all, she understood what was happening. She had the good sense to ask herself why things hadn't worked first time — and come up with the right answers. It wasn't Tangle's fault, it was hers for putting him in that position and then failing to communicate her wishes to him as clearly as she wanted. Her attitude impressed me deeply and the memory of it stayed with me afterwards. She made me realise, perhaps for the first time, how crucial it is to remember to avoid the blame game with your dogs.

In the ensuing weeks and months, I got to know Maria better. It was a measure of her dedication and determination to keep pushing the boundaries of her knowledge that she enrolled on one of my courses. She wasn't the first professional trainer to enrol on the course. As with the others who had visited me, I entirely respected the methods they were required to use professionally. All I did was to suggest different ways of thinking about things.

Maria embraced many of my ideas wholeheartedly. Back at Oxford, there were still those who wanted to stick to more traditional methods. But talking as I did to Maria on a regular basis, I was pleased to hear there were one or two who had adopted my methods as well.

I remained an active supporter of Dogs for the Disabled and revisited Oxford not long afterwards. Naturally, I asked after Tangle, and Maria told me he was now living in a partnership with a disabled person, performing all the jobs he'd been prepared for — and one or two others besides.

"He's doing brilliantly," she told me. From the moment I met the pair of them I had sensed that, with a trainer like Maria, Tangle was never going to do anything but.

HAPPY FAMILIES

Why great owners are fun owners

As far as I am concerned, there really is no point in taking on the responsibility of a dog unless you are going to enjoy it. It should be a pleasure not a punishment, for both human and canine. Yet I come across many people who — for whatever reason — seem to regard the role like some terrible cross they have to bear. It is as if they are doing the job under sufferance.

We've all seen these owners looking miserable while they are out and about with their dogs. I've met quite a few who have told me they regard walking their dog each day as a terrible chore. My response is always the same: if looking after your dog is such a pain then why did you take it on in the first place?

Apart from anything else, sharing a few moments of daily fun with your best friend is one of the most positive things you can do for your dog. Most people know that dogs acquire an important part of their education through playing as puppies. But what many don't realise is that play remains an important element throughout a dog's life. The importance of playing and generally leading as joyful a life as you can with your dog cannot be overestimated. Two very different owners were instrumental in teaching me just how central a part of a dog's life this is.

I visited Tony as part of the television series I did, *The Dog Listener*. Tony lived with his wife and their two big dogs, Casper, a four-year-old Rottweiler and Ben, a ten-year-old golden retriever. Casper suffered badly from separation anxiety and he would tear up the house whenever Tony left him alone there. Casper's favourite comfy chair had borne the brunt of his insecurity and, when I visited, it was a mass of torn material, exposed wood and foam.

The case had been a relatively straightforward one. Tony needed to get Casper to accept that, as leader, he was free to come and go from the house as and when he pleased. After introducing the basic principles of my method, I got Tony to work on what I call "gesture leaving", whereby he kept leaving by the front door, then returning after a longer and longer period. This soon had the desired effect, with Casper calming down considerably as he got the message that he was being relieved of the pressures of leadership.

But it was what happened afterwards that really struck Tony and me. With the atmosphere in the house changing noticeably, Ben suddenly walked over to Casper and put his paw on his nose. Rather than rejecting this, Casper turned to Ben and made a playful grab at him. Within a few seconds Ben flipped on to his back, Casper performed a mini somersault and the pair

130

of them were rolling around, enjoying a really lively bit of rough and tumble on the floor.

Tony's face was a picture, I recall. "They've never, ever done that before," he said to me, his jaw almost ready to hit the floor.

I knew that having the burden of leadership lifted is a liberating experience for dogs and I'd seen dogs relax and learn to enjoy themselves quickly before. But even I was taken aback by the suddenness of this transformation. It was as if a huge weight had been lifted off their shoulders and they were celebrating in the most spontaneous and natural way they could imagine.

The change in Casper and Ben was so dramatic in the days and weeks that followed, that Tony had to consign the pair of them to the garden to play. "They were smashing up the place they were getting so lively," he laughed when I spoke to him.

"That's how dogs behave when they're off duty," I told Tony. "They have both been too wrapped up in looking after you and the rest of the house even to consider having any fun before. Let them enjoy it." It was a moment that underlined my belief in the power of play.

It was not long after dealing with Casper, Ben and Tony, that a lady called Tracey and her dog Mabel reinforced the power of play even more.

I will never forget the way Tracey introduced herself when she called me at home one day. "Please don't laugh at me, but I'm worried about my dog because she can't play," she said.

The dog she was talking about was Mabel, a rescued crossbreed she'd acquired a few months earlier. She had heard about Mabel through her contacts at the local rescue centre. Mabel had been found abandoned in a shed on a rural property near her home in Kent. Apparently the owners had moved and decided to leave her there without any food or water. She was in a pretty poor state when someone had come across her by accident. The rescue centre did a sterling job in rebuilding her, but she was still far from recovered when she arrived at Tracey's house. Her coat was still in a very poor condition, she had scabs and, worst of all, an infection under her toes caused by a grass seed that had got lodged there.

The scars were not just physical, however. Emotionally, Mabel was a deeply damaged dog. She would jump around a lot and grow very agitated when a stranger came to the door. She was clearly scared of people — and occasionally of objects. If Tracey had anything attached to a stick, such as a brush or a mop, or a rake in the garden, Mabel would recoil, looking terrified. It wasn't hard to work out that she must have been beaten with something of this kind by her previous owners.

Tracey knew that it was going to be a long, slow road to recovery. As an experienced dog person, this was something she was prepared to accept. But what worried her most was the way in which Mabel seemed unwilling or unable to relax.

Tracey had another dog, Mac, a really fun character that she had also rescued a few years earlier. He would regularly lower his front legs in front of Mabel, sticking his bottom in the air and wagging his tail as if to say, "Come on, let's have some fun." But each time he did this, Mabel would simply run away.

At first, Tracey simply put this down to Mabel's troubled past. Quite rightly, she figured that Mabel was still wary of others, had not settled in properly and had yet to shake off the physical effects of her mistreatment at the hands of her previous owners. So, as Tracey spent the first few months gently easing her along, she didn't worry overmuch about this. In any case, Mabel's foot infection required a small operation so she was incapacitated for part of this time. But, as time wore on and Mabel continued to shun Mac's invitations to play, Tracey sensed that there was something seriously wrong. And it was at this point that she called me in.

Great owners tend to possess a sort of sixth sense about their dogs. Tracey instinctively knew there was something important missing from Mabel's life. She was willing to risk being laughed at in order to discover what it was, and that impressed me immediately. "I hope you don't think I'm silly," she kept saying to me during our first conversation. The first thing I did was to praise her rather than laugh at her. "You will never hear me say a word against an owner who wants their dog to enjoy life more," I told her. "You mustn't feel you're silly at all."

Encouraging a sense of fun and play is central to my method. A disciplined approach, in which owners remain in control of playtime, is essential. But by capitalising on their natural playful instincts, owners can make huge progress in rebuilding a dog's self-esteem and trust in the world, particularly in the case of damaged dogs where the freedom and joy a dog experiences during play can have a wonderfully restorative effect. Naturally, if — as in Mabel's case — the dog concerned has been hurt by people in the past, this is something that is going to have to evolve slowly.

When I visited Tracey, I began by explaining to her the root cause of Mabel's unwillingness to relax with Mac. Every dog manifests its feelings of stress in different ways. In Mabel's case, she was not going to be able to play while she still regarded herself as leader of her pack and was agitated about the responsibility that brought with it. I compared the situation to a parent in charge of a child. Would you just walk out to play a round of golf and leave your baby on its own at home? Of course not. You would only be able to play when you felt you were off duty. So our job was to persuade Mabel she was off duty.

We then proceeded in the normal way, implementing the four key elements of my method and establishing Tracey as leader.

Three days after I'd visited Tracey the phone went.

"I couldn't wait any longer to call you," Tracey said, sniffling a little.

She told me that Mabel's progress had been phenomenal. Her personality had changed dramatically, becoming a much calmer, less wary, generally happier dog. The previous evening she heard

Mabel issue a huge sigh, something she'd never heard before.

The most dramatic development had come that morning, however. It was a lovely day and, as usual, Tracey had let the two dogs out into the garden. Mac went through his "let's play" ritual once more, crouching down, sticking his bottom in the air and wagging his tail. He then jumped in the air, spun round and run off to the other end of the garden. To Tracey's delight, Mabel had immediately scampered off after him. Even better was what happened at the other end of the garden. There Mabel reversed the roles, crouching down before jumping up and haring off with Mac now in hot pursuit. This game of chase had been going on for the best part of an hour.

"I'm looking out of the window into the garden now and the two of them are still playing together," she told me, through the tears. "I don't know when it's going to end and I don't care."

I must admit it was one of those magic moments, but there were more to come. A few weeks passed and I didn't hear from Tracey. I had been so taken by her and the work she was doing with Mabel that I couldn't bear not knowing how they were doing, so I rang her.

"You must be telepathic," she told me. "I was about to call you when I stopped crying."

As you might have already gathered, Tracey was someone who was quick to tears! Once more her dogs had provided her with something that had moved her enormously. Mabel's progress had continued over the past weeks. One of the most pleasing things to Tracey was the way the dog had now found the confidence to let herself be tickled on the tummy.

Again, it was something Tracey had built up slowly, but now it was an almost daily part of their routine together. All Tracey needed to do was rub her hands gently on the floor and Mabel would come bounding over, flip herself on to her back and lie there having her tummy rubbed.

But the most significant development of all had come in the garden. Mabel still hadn't taken to playing with a ball. As I told Tracey, this may well have been purely a matter of preference. Not every dog enjoys the same physical activities. By contrast, however, Mabel had become a huge fan of agility work, and in particular jumping over obstacles. At first, Tracey used small items from the house to make impromptu hurdles which Mabel would endlessly hop over. But, as her abilities improved, Tracey moved on to building small fences using wastepaper baskets and a kitchen broom. Mabel was now jumping over these obstacles, maybe twelve to eighteen inches high, with ease.

The moment that really struck me, came when Tracey told me how she'd begun using all manner of household items to build Mabel's obstacles. "I've even used a broom and a rake to make a bar for her to jump," she told me one day. This, to me, was a revelation, real proof that with hard work all owners can help their dogs overcome even the most deeply ingrained fears. A few months earlier, the mere sight of these tools had sent Mabel into a panic. Now the instruments of fear had been transformed into instruments of fun.

COMETH THE HOUR

Why great owners
rise to the occasion

As Shakespeare put it, some are born great, some achieve greatness, and some have greatness thrust upon them. In the course of my career, I've come across owners who fall into all these categories. I've know a few people whose dog skills were completely natural. It was as if they had been blessed with a God-given gift that made dogs comfortable in their presence. For most people, myself included, successful ownership has been achieved through sheer hard work and dedication.

Occasionally I have also encountered some who became great dog owners almost by accident. They had greatness thrust upon them. Owning a dog was certainly not something Blair and Stella had factored into their busy lives. When fate called on them, however, they proved themselves more than up to the challenge.

Blair was a journalist and presenter who had arrived from London to work on the local radio station in Hull, BBC Radio Humberside. His wife Stella was an optician, trying to establish her own practice in the area.

Blair and Stella decided to rent a lovely cottage on farmland near the town of Beverley. They fell in love with the place almost instantly. It looked like an idyllic home, a place that seemed to offer everything: rolling open fields, birdsong and, above all, a peaceful escape from their busy professional lives.

In fact, there was only one blemish, at the far end of the land adjoining the cottage there was a rather rundown-looking dog. A cross between a lurcher and a deerhound, it was grey, speckled and very, very lean. It was attached to a rickety shed by a ten-foot chain.

"What's he doing there?" Blair asked the farmer.

The farmer seemed surprised that he had even noticed him.

"Oh, him, that's Scooby, he just lives there," the farmer said.

Blair's journalistic instincts meant he couldn't just leave it at that. He quizzed the farmer a bit more and found out that he'd been put there as a guard dog. He'd been there since he was a puppy, but he was now seven years old — it was clear he was neglected terribly. There was a lot of mess around him and the shed itself was barely deserving of that description.

Blair was not someone who took an interest in dogs. But even he was flabbergasted by this. He and Stella had already decided to take the cottage and he didn't want to insult the farmer to his face. "The poor thing's been living like that for seven years, that's unbelievable," he said to Stella out of the farmer's earshot.

Almost as soon as they moved in, Blair found himself drawn towards Scooby. "I can't leave the old fella there like that," he told Stella. "He's a smashing-looking dog, he deserves better."

He was appalled at the conditions he lived in, so began by doing what he could to patch up Scooby's pathetic little shed. The flimsy construction was more draught than shed. There was a huge door where the wind whistled in, so Blair's first act was to tack on pieces of hessian sacking to block out the draught.

The farmer only fed Scooby occasionally, and even then with scraps. Blair didn't want to antagonise his landlord by being obvious about it, but when he knew the coast was clear he would give Scooby a bowl of dog food. Unsurprisingly, Blair didn't have to wait long for his new-found friend to wolf it down.

After a few weeks, Scooby's spirits had lifted noticeably. When Blair had first met him his eyes were dead. Now whenever Blair came near him he would wag his tail excitedly and there was a brightness in his eyes. Blair sensed that he had ignited a little bit of hope in Scooby's heart — and he had no intention of seeing it extinguished.

The thing that upset Blair more than anything else was seeing such a big, athletic dog being denied any freedom. One day he approached the farmer to ask him whether he ever let Scooby off the leash. Again he couldn't have seemed less interested. "Naaah, he just runs away," he said with a dismissive wave of his hand.

Blair was determined to find out a bit more and he discovered that on a couple of occasions someone had

140

slipped on to the farm and let Scooby loose from his chains. The farmer suspected "some animal rights woman" in the nearby village. "Good for her," Blair said inwardly. It turned out that on one occasion Scooby had run ten miles before being found by the police.

A few days later, Blair bit the bullet and asked the farmer whether he'd mind him taking Scooby on a walk every now and again. "I'd be sure to keep him on a tight leash," he said. "I won't let him run off." The farmer was a bit taken aback, but as ever his interest was short-lived.

"As long as you know if you lose him, it'll be up to you to bring him back," he muttered.

Soon Blair was taking Scooby out almost daily on walks through the surrounding fields. He put him on as long a lead as possible to give him as much of a run as he could. He didn't let him run free — not just yet, anyway.

Over the following weeks and months, Blair and Scooby became the best of pals. Blair's job involved unpredictable hours, but he made sure he fitted in some time with Scooby each day, even if it was first thing in the morning or last thing at night.

The one line he and Stella could not cross, however, was taking Scooby into the house. The farmer had made it a strict condition of the tenancy that no animals were allowed in the house. When they had taken on the house, this had suited Stella and Blair down to the ground. Now it was a frustration, especially when summer turned to winter. Blair and

Stella had to shut the curtains at night because they couldn't bear to think they might see Scooby coping with the cutting winds blowing in off the North Sea. Blair felt so bad that he bought a huge piece of tarpaulin that he used to patch every tiny hole in the shed.

By the time their first year at the farm was drawing to a close, both Stella and Blair's careers were on the up and up. Rather than renewing the tenancy, they decided to buy a home instead. Having made one big decision, they then made another. One morning Blair approached the farmer and asked him whether they could take Scooby with them.

Even this failed to get much of a response. "If you want," he said.

"Don't you want anything for him?" Blair asked.

"No, you're all right. He's getting old now, you're doing me a favour taking him off my hands," the farmer said.

I'd known Blair through my work on phone-ins on Radio Humberside. I had spoken to him about Scooby before and, as he and Stella prepared to take him into their home, I did so again. I laid it on the line and my message was bleak. Given the awful way he'd been treated for the first seven years of his life, Scooby was always going to be scarred to a certain extent. This didn't deter them at all.

Over the course of the following weeks and months they demonstrated many great qualities. Their selflessness was among the most impressive things. Before they had used to travel a great deal, taking regular foreign holidays and socialising a lot. With Scooby to care for, both made sure they were home much more. They were also realistic about what they could achieve. Scooby had spent the formative years of his life forcefully prevented from moving more than ten feet. It had been little wonder that he'd just run for it whenever he had the opportunity. That "flight" instinct was still strong within him, so Blair and Stella knew they had to watch him carefully. One of Blair's first jobs was to make good the fencing around the property.

Even this didn't deter him from running away on one occasion when someone left the gate open. Scooby's disappearance panicked Blair and Stella who rang the police. When the officer asked them to describe the dog, Blair just said: "It's that lurcher that used to live at that farm on the edge of Beverley." "Oh we know him," the officer said with a chuckle.

As it happened the police weren't needed this time — Scooby returned home within a couple of hours.

His escape was in no way a reflection of the treatment he was getting from his new owners. I visited them there during their early days and witnessed a picture of domestic bliss that would have warmed the coldest heart. Scooby looked like a dog that had died and gone to heaven. The eyes that had once been so dead and devoid of emotion were now full of contentment. The house was scattered with bean bags, on which he would enjoy regular naps. There was one in the kitchen, one in the sitting room and another one — the biggest of all — on the top of the stairs opposite Blair and Stella's bedroom, where Scooby slept.

It was obvious that Scooby and Blair had become inseparable. Stella told me that if Blair went outside to the garden, Scooby would climb up on to the window and press his nose against the glass, crying as he did so. I remember one day I was sitting chatting to Blair in the kitchen. He is a tall man and had his legs stretched out in front of his chair. Slowly but surely, Scooby slid under his legs, then forced his way through Blair's crossed ankles so as to coil himself around his pal.

"I never knew a dog could be such a good friend," Blair told me once.

Only once did I detect a hint of sadness in his voice when talking about what they'd done. Soon after he'd moved away from the farm, Blair had been talking to someone in the village who knew his former landlord.

"I bet you anything he's got another dog chained up there now," she said, shaking her head disapprovingly. "That's the way people like him are."

Blair admitted to me that he'd never had the courage to go back to the farm to see if that was true. "It broke my heart to see Scooby like that, I don't know if I could take it to see another dog treated that way," he said.

Scooby lived with Stella and Blair for six years. During that time they welcomed their first child into the world, baby Hannah. Scooby got on with the new arrival perfectly. As he got older, however, he developed severe arthritis and had to be given a lot of medication to ease the pain.

Blair and I remained close professionally too. I often appeared on his radio shows and when I did, always asked after Scooby. One morning I was getting ready to

144

go on when his producer came up to me and said, "Oh, by the way, Jan, don't ask him how Scooby is, he died a couple of weeks ago."

Blair was too upset to talk about it on air, but we did chat later on. He told me he had been hit hard by the loss at first. The wounds were still raw, but he had slowly begun to look back on Scooby as something of a gift in his life. He'd never had a dog before and said he couldn't imagine having one again. "He was a one-off," he said, with a faraway smile, memories of Scooby obviously filling his head.

As we chatted, I told him how much I'd admired the way he'd dealt with Scooby and the whole situation. I told him he had also made me realise something I had not really seen before.

There is — it has to be said — a lot of snobbishness about dog ownership. There are some people who believe only a privileged few are fit to own dogs, that unless you have years of experience and an encyclopaedic knowledge of the canine world you should not be allowed to share your life with even the most mixed-up crossbreeds. This is plainly nonsense — and Blair, to me, was living proof of that.

Scooby had arrived in his life purely by chance. He was not someone with a particular interest in dogs, nor did he fit the perfect profile of someone with the right setup to care for a dog.

Yet despite a difficult set of circumstances, he had risen to the occasion in a way that would have put all but the most dedicated owners to shame. By displaying sheer goodness and humanity — not to mention an instinctive understanding of dogs — he had given a very unhappy and abused dog a longer, happier life. Even if he never had another dog in his life, I told him he had made a difference for at least one canine in this world. "Cometh the hour, cometh the man," goes the old saying. In Scooby's hour of need, Blair had been the man who came to his aid, and for that he has every reason to be proud of himself.

THE BEST DOG COMES HOME WITH US

The importance of owning dogs for the right reasons

Dogs have always been seen as something of a fashion accessory by some, but it seems to me that nowadays more people than ever view them like this. Far too many owners are concerned with what their dog says about them. I'm growing heartily sick of the sight of so-called celebrities turning up at events with their dogs in tow, using their pet as nothing more than another photo opportunity, a way to get the world to "look at me". It is as if everyone sees themselves in some kind of beauty competition and they want their dogs — and by extension, themselves — to be seen as something special.

While I am fortunate enough to encounter more than my share of selfless owners — accidental heroes like Blair — it is also my misfortune every now and again to encounter less admirable individuals. These people want to improve their pet's behaviour not for the dog's sake, but because it reflects badly on them, because it embarrasses them.

147

Whenever I do, I remind them that just as there is no such thing as a perfect human being, neither is there such a thing as a perfect dog. Above all, I remind them of a saying I learned from a truly great dog owner called Bert Green: "The best dog comes home with us."

I've been fortunate enough to meet a lot of wonderful people in the dog world, many of whom have passed on words of wisdom that have stayed with me. I sometimes think of myself as a gem collector, and these people as dispensers of jewels. No one offered me more priceless insights than Bert.

I first met Bert in the spring of 1975. I had just decided to dip my toe into the waters of the competitive show world and had arrived at my first major event, an English springer spaniels championship in Lough-borough, with my dog Lady. It was an overwhelming — and slightly baffling — experience. There were more than two hundred dogs there, spaniels of all ages, from six-month-old puppies to veterans.

I had never met Bert before, but knew of him because he owned Scott, Lady's father. I was eager to make friends so went over to talk to him and his wife Gwen, who was there with him. Bert was a tall, willowy figure, already in his seventies by then. He was more than willing to talk me through the intricacies of the event. "There's an awful lot to learn," he said — and he wasn't wrong.

I remember Bert going off into a detailed dissection of what the judges were looking for. He talked about

148

the importance of a good "reach of neck" and a dog that "moves with drive". He wasn't trying to be clever, he was genuinely trying to help, but I really didn't have a clue what it all meant. He might as well have been talking in Mandarin. It reminded me of the strange lexicon of terms and jargon I had to get used to when I joined the WRNS, as an eighteen-year-old in the 1960s.

Gwen spotted this and intervened after a while. "Leave her alone, love. You're giving her a headache," she said, chuckling.

"Of course, it must be a bit intimidating," he said. "But if there's ever anything I can do to help, don't be afraid to ask."

They were such a lovely couple I really took to them immediately. Their kindness only added to the excitement and appeal of the day. When I got home that night, I thought to myself: "That's fun, I'll do that again."

One of the first things I learned about the show world was that it consisted of a relatively small group of people. As I began taking Lady around the country, I kept seeing the same familiar faces all over again. Bert's became the most familiar face of all. He had been very diplomatic in assessing Lady. "You'll have a lot of fun with her, but don't expect too much," he said. It was only later I realised what he meant. As a pet she was a fantastic dog, but she was never realistically going to be a prizewinner at shows.

I knew that if I was going to achieve that sort of success it would be by breeding better examples of the breed. When I told him this, Bert became even more of a mentor to me — to my amazement and delight he offered me one of his dogs, Donna, to begin a line of English springers. To me it was a huge compliment that he would even consider offering me one of his prized dogs. As we made the preparations to collect Donna we got to know each other even better, and it was then that he came up with his first piece of really important advice.

The goal of anyone who breeds a dog should be to improve the breed of which that dog is a member. Every breed has a standard, a set of guidelines as to its ideal size, proportions, bone structure and temperament. In breeding terms, the quality of the English springer spaniels was as high then as it had been in a long time. One day we were talking and Bert said to me, "I doubt you'll do the breed any good, but don't do it any bloody harm."

In general terms, I understood what he meant here immediately. He was saying: "Be sure to choose with care the dogs from which you breed". He wanted me to understand the responsibility of what I was about to undertake, and I took his words to heart, exercising all the care I could over the following years. It was in large part because of Bert's advice that I managed to produce some exceptional dogs that didn't do the breed any harm in the years that followed.

Bert was a man with an opinion on most matters canine. It was his views on the competitive nature of the show world that resonated longest and loudest in my mind. His love of dogs ran deep, and he achieved a lot of success with both Scott and another dog Sherry.

150

All owners love winning, but for Bert it was only ever a bonus when this happened. To him the enjoyment of being amongst people with a shared passion and seeing his dogs appreciated was enough. He despised those who were in it for what he called "their own glory".

We were talking about this once, when he said to me, "Remember, Jan, the best dog comes home with us." I didn't understand this instantly, but the more I got into the show world the more clearly I began to see what he meant.

Dog shows are no different from any other area where people compete. You witness human nature at its best — and occasionally its worst too. As the dogs I bred took me further into the show world, I saw some things that made my blood turn cold. I saw dogs yanked all over the ring when they didn't deliver their owners the winning rosettes they had expected. I saw dogs thrown on to benches afterwards, as if they'd done something wrong. I was standing next to a young girl once, and was giving one of my dogs some food reward at the end of its turn going round the arena. This young girl's dog looked over, salivating at the sight and smell of the food.

I wouldn't have dreamed of offering the food without the owner's permission so caught her eye and asked: "Would it be all right?"

"No, she only gets something nice if she wins," she said to me.

To me, seeing dogs treated in this way was deeply depressing. And over the following years I saw it not

151

just in dog shows, but in obedience and agility competitions, police dog competitions, even in sheepdog trials. Whilst the majority treated their dogs gently and with respect, there was always a large minority that were brisk or downright cruel with their dogs if they didn't live up to their expectations. To me, it was clear they were participating for their own egotistical reasons rather than for the good of the dog.

Bert Green remained an important influence on me for many years. Among his many great qualities was his realism. As he reached his late seventies, he was still knowledgeable enough to have carried on breeding, but he knew that he wouldn't be around long enough to see the next generation of dogs through the twelve or fourteen years of their lifespan, so he retired. He died four years later, followed — all too soon afterwards — by Gwen.

It has only been in recent years that I've really come to see how deep Bert's insights were and how they apply far beyond the show world.

His belief that we shouldn't do our dogs any harm in breeding them appears more prescient than ever. There seem to be more people than ever willing to breed dogs without proper consideration, something I will discuss in the following chapter. His most profound thought, however, was encapsulated in that favourite phrase of his.

The truth is that all our dogs are special, and it doesn't matter whether one person or a million appreciate that. We should enjoy our dogs for what they are, not for what they say about us or our status. In many ways, it is as important a message as any other. We should all remember that the best dog always comes home with us.

BETTER HAPPY
THAN RICH

Why great owners understand
the real value of dogs

As men like Bert Green never tired of telling me, our responsibilities as dog owners are great. What I have come to realise more and more is that these responsibilities begin even before a dog joins a new home.

Whether you are a new owner or, as I am occasionally, someone who has bred a litter of puppies and is looking to find them a home, you have a duty to protect the species about which you care so deeply. And your primary duty is to ensure your dogs end up in the right hands. Sadly, it is a view not shared by everyone.

People own and breed dogs for a myriad reasons: they can provide us with companionship, affection or simply a jolly good reason to get out into the fresh air each day. Unfortunately, they can also provide financial gain — and money, in the dog world as everywhere else, is the root of all evil.

If there is one subject guaranteed to get me hot under the collar, it is the issue of unscrupulous breeders, the so-called "puppy farmers". It has been my misfortune to have come across a number of these people over the years. All of them were get-rich-quick merchants, all too willing to churn out scores of dogs each year, packing the poor creatures into upturned tea chests and selling them to the first person who waved enough money in their direction. As far as I'm concerned, they are the major reason why our sanctuaries and rescue centres are so full of unwanted dogs. I would like to explain my thoughts about how they should be dealt with, but I fear they might be unprintable.

In many ways, puppy farmers are the definition of the very worst kind of dog owner. They are concerned purely with profit and have no regard whatsoever for the welfare of the dogs — or, for that matter, their owners. The harm they do to the breeds they mass-produce does not bear thinking about. They are, as my grandmother used to say, the sort of people who know the price of everything and the value of nothing.

If I know the value of dogs, it is down to the wisdom provided to me by a group of people in my past. Men like Bert Green taught me much, but no one was more influential in this respect than Evelyn Needham. To me, Evelyn was the polar opposite of the puppy farmer — someone who understood the real value of dogs, and wouldn't compromise her principles at any price. She played a pivotal role in moulding my opinions. We would all do well to take a leaf out of her book.

★ ★ ★

I came across Evelyn when I was living in Firsby. She and her husband John kept a boarding kennel and smallholding near the seaside resort of Skegness where they also bred the most magnificent Irish setters.

I'd met them first during my forays into the show world, where their setters were regular prizewinners. As I got to know them better, I used to visit them weekly, mainly to buy milk from their small herd of goats, which I fed to my own dogs. I used to thoroughly enjoy popping in to see Evelyn and John. Their kennels were always immaculate and they took such pride in their dogs. I learned a great deal from them — both directly and indirectly.

The first insight they gave me came one summer's evening. As usual, I'd collected a few bags of goat's milk from John and was walking back across the yard when I saw Evelyn in conversation with a family. It only took a cursory look at their T-shirts, shorts and sandals to work out they were holidaymakers.

It was inevitable that John and Evelyn's boarding kennels would attract tourists. To begin with, they were situated on a main road, leading into Skegness. Evelyn and John also had a large sign, with the silhouette of a handsome Irish setter on it, hanging outside. They also had a smaller sign, indicating their opening and closing times, but that hadn't deterred their visitors. Irish setters have always been popular dogs, but they were particularly in vogue at that time. From the conversation, it was clear what was going on.

"We'll pay you well over the odds. Our kids have set their heart on one," I heard the father say. Things got mildly heated at one stage, with the father waving his arms in the air. Evelyn kept her composure, however, and just smiled nicely. This went on for about ten minutes or so, with the father's face reddening. Eventually, the family began making their way back to their car, talking animatedly as they went. Evelyn's voice seemed to raise itself as they went. "Enjoy your holiday, and when you get back home give me a call," she said.

Once she'd waved them out of the yard and closed the gate behind them, she turned back to John and me.

"We'll not be hearing from them again," she smiled.

Evelyn explained that the family had turned up expecting to be able to buy an Irish setter puppy there and then. A good Irish setter could fetch between £100 and £150, a lot of money in the 1970s. John and Evelyn's dogs were amongst the finest examples of the breed in the country and could have fetched much more than that. The father had clearly been willing to pay whatever it took. But Evelyn had done what she always did.

"I told them that I could give them the name of a good breeder in their area. If they still felt the same way after their holiday, they could give me a call and I'd pass on the number," she said, with a knowing smile.

"I get two or three visits like these a week but they never call back," she said. "They just call on a whim."

I had begun breeding dogs myself at this point. My own springer Donna was carrying her first litter, but so far I'd thought more about my friend Bert Green's advice and the selection of a mate for my dog than the

157

sale of the pups she'd produce. Listening to Evelyn made me aware of how careful you had to be about whom you sold a dog to.

"These people come here on a whim," she said. "They see the sign with the setter on it and think 'Oh, that'd be nice.' They give it no more thought than buying a sun hat on the beach at Skegness."

Then she said something I'll never forget. "We'll never be rich, will we, John? But we'll be happy," she said.

Evelyn and John were quiet, gentle people. They were not the type to pontificate or preach — they preferred to let people work things out for themselves. It was shortly after seeing Evelyn deal with those visitors, that she orchestrated — perhaps deliberately, perhaps not — an experience that just underlined how right she was.

I had been feeding my dogs tripe at the time and was looking for someone who could provide me with a regular supply. Talking to Evelyn one evening, I mentioned the name of a lady who was supposedly selling it cheap.

When I mentioned her name, Evelyn gave a knowing sort of smile.

"Oh, you know her, do you?" I said.

"I don't know her, but let's say I've heard of her," she replied.

"What do you mean?" I said.

"Oh, it's best if you meet her yourself. I'm sure you'll find her interesting," Evelyn said.

So it was that a few days later I went to visit this lady at her kennels a few miles away.

At the time, by far the most fashionable dog in England was the Afghan hound. I think it was a television advert or a programme of the time that had made them popular. Whatever the reason, this lady was clearly capitalising on this vogue.

Everywhere I looked there were Afghans of varying shades, sizes and both sexes. "Goodness," I said. "How do you cope with all these?"

"Oooh, they're not here for long. Can't breed enough of them," she said.

I asked her how much they fetched and was shocked when she told me around £250 a puppy. At the time £70 was a good price for a good dog.

My sense of shock only deepened as I looked around. How anyone would have paid £250 for a dog that had come from these kennels was beyond me. The kennels looked as if they hadn't been cleaned in months. The stench was awful. Just as bad, they were very cheaply constructed and weren't properly sheltered.

Inevitably, this had had an effect on the dogs, many of whom were in a really poor condition. Afghans have magnificent coats, a covering of fine, silky hair that takes some looking after. The state of these dogs' coats was pitiful. Many of them had chunks of hair missing. I left there unable to quite believe what I'd seen.

It wasn't long afterwards that I saw Evelyn and John again.

"Did you get your tripe from that woman?" Evelyn asked, that knowing look on her face once more.

"Oh, don't," I said. "Did you know about her?"

The look on her face said it all.

"Why didn't you warn me?" I said.

"It's not for me to say who you do business with," she said. "I thought you'd best make a judgment for yourself."

But John wasn't quite so diplomatic.

"I told you Jan wouldn't stick it there for five minutes," he said. "The place is a disgrace."

I couldn't have agreed more.

If Evelyn's aim had been to show me how *not* to breed dogs then she'd succeeded. I never returned to those kennels and, unlike Evelyn, never shied away from telling the truth on the rare occasions when anyone mentioned them.

On the other hand, my respect for Evelyn and John had only deepened. I remained close to them for a long time. And even when I moved away from the area and lost contact I tried to live by the principles to which they introduced me, being extremely careful about choosing the people to whom I sell my dogs.

On more than one occasion, I've turned people away. Sometimes it has been the way they are around dogs generally. Dogs have highly developed senses and can often tell a great deal about a person by the aura they give off. Several times I have decided against placing dogs on the basis of my own dogs' reaction. On other occasion, I've simply known they were wrong.

Recently I met a lady whose only concern seemed to be the width of the blaze on the dog's face or the depth of the brown in its liver colouring. "I'm sorry you seem to be looking for a designer dog," I told her. "I don't have any of those here."

Whatever our position within the dog-owning world, ours is a huge and onerous responsibility. As breeders we have a duty to make sure our dogs end up in the right hands. And as owners, each and every one of us should look at our motives for taking on a dog. Evelyn was an important influence in forging my philosophy on this. Owners everywhere would do well to reflect on her wisdom.

GIVE A DOG A GOOD NAME

Why great owners don't pigeonhole their dogs

To most dog lovers, the idea that each dog is an individual with its own distinct personality is so obvious that it hardly needs stating. Yet I am constantly amazed and saddened by the number of people I come across who don't think this way at all, so many people pigeonhole dogs into stereotypes, mostly according to breed. We have all heard these self-appointed experts at work, their opinions usually preceded by phrases such as "everyone knows": "Everyone knows all beagles are a bit wilful", "Everyone knows all Dobermans are aggressive", "Everyone knows all springers are loopy", and so on.

Of course, it's nonsense. To say that every single German shepherd is aggressive or that every Pekinese is petulant makes about as much sense as saying that every Brazilian is a good footballer or every Welshman can sing. In humans, such generalisations are plain daft. The problem when this sort of blinkered thinking is applied to dogs, is not just that it is misleading, it can

162

be downright dangerous. Once a dog has been given a bad name, it is extremely hard to clear that reputation.

No good owner is going to think this way. But what has distinguished the great owners I've come across has been their willingness to confront this sort of thinking head on. This is something that can require a lot of guts, something "Peter", a handler with the RAF, was certainly not lacking.

I have nothing but respect for our armed forces. Having been in the WRNS myself as a young woman, I appreciate and value the job our sailors, soldiers and airmen do for the country. It therefore grieves me to criticise them but, in this case, I have no choice. To my mind, the armed forces are home to some of the most deeply entrenched, old-fashioned ideas about dogs.

Peter worked at an air base in the south of England, where he was involved in security. He needed a dog to accompany him on his security rounds and had gone to one of the services' dog-training centres. These training schemes are intense, lasting only a few weeks. The services tend to be given unwanted dogs, mostly aged between eighteen and twenty-four months. I am not going to pretend I approve of the way they go about things, which is based on the traditional enforcement methods. I appreciate they have a job to do and the pressure they are under, but I just don't agree with the treatment given in this environment to dogs that do not immediately bend to their handler's will.

Apart from my own experience in the WRNS, I'd had first-hand experience of the Army's attitude to dog training not long before I met Peter, when I was invited to a dinner at a dog-training camp. Before the evening began I'd been given a tour of the kennels and had been depressed by the confusion and anxiety I saw in the dogs' eyes. Talking to the handlers over dinner it was easy to see why they looked so mixed-up and intimidated.

No one worked with the same dog all the time, so there was no chance to build a relationship between handler and dog, let alone remove the role of leader from the dogs. What was worse, however, was the harsh treatment meted out to the dogs; one female handler explained to me that she was expected to train the dogs by using force. At times they would pull so hard on a choke chain that the dog's feet would come off the ground.

When I suggested this was, in my view, close to abuse, she and her fellow students were quick to explain the reality to me. This was the Forces' way of training and this was the way its instructors had worked for many years. To defy this regimented approach would be to bring the whole authority of the top brass down on them. "I know you're way's a more humane way, but we'd seal our own fate if we did it here," one handler told me.

It was this approach that Peter had come up against as well. Peter had begun working with a group of dogs, but had become drawn to a German shepherd. It was a highly intelligent dog, and for this reason it wasn't responding well to the harsh training regime. Things had come to a head when it had bitten two separate handlers. To the military mindset, such open defiance was intolerable. The dog's behaviour confirmed two stereotypical views: firstly, this was a German shepherd — a dog that everyone knows is aggressive; even more damning, this was a German shepherd who had "turned". And, as everyone supposedly knows, once a dog has turned there is literally no turning back. Peter learned that a decision had been made about the dog. The armed forces describe the process as "euthanising" the dog. What they mean is killing it.

As a breed, German shepherds get a particularly raw deal. Knowledgeable people recognise them as among the most intelligent of all dogs. The Guide Dogs for the Blind organisation would like to use the breed as much as they use Labradors. Yet they know the public recoil from this breed because of its undeserved reputation as aggressive, attack dogs. To me, the problem really lies with irresponsible breeders who have not been careful in the dogs they have chosen. We are the cause and the rare aggressive German shepherd is the effect. We have given the dog its bad name.

The easiest thing to do would have been to accept this, to stick with the norm. But Peter wasn't a normal dog handler, he was someone who thought for himself. He knew this was a good dog and he was determined to reverse the stereotypical view of it. He simply wasn't going to let his superiors put this dog down — at least, not without a fight.

I met Peter at one of my courses, where he impressed me with the faith he had in his dog. "I know he's the best dog there, but no one's willing to see him as anything other than trouble," he told me. He was determined to change that.

Back at the training school, Peter went over the instructors' heads and approached one of his superiors. He asked the officer to trust him and keep an open mind. In return, he promised to do everything in his power to convince the camp this dog didn't deserve to be on death row. He knew the dog was drinking at the Last Chance Saloon and he was its last hope.

Peter began working in secret. He was helped by the fact that none of the other handlers wanted to work with this dog. The dogs were generally let out of their kennels for breakfast and exercise at 7.30, so Peter began getting there at 6.30. He began by changing the breakfast routine. Rather than just plonking the breakfast bowl down in front of the dog, he used my gesture-eating technique. He arrived outside the kennel with the bowl in one hand and a biscuit or a piece of toast in the other. With the dog watching him he finished eating his snack before placing the bowl down, thereby underlining in the clearest possible language that — as leader — he was in charge of the food supply and the order in which it was dispensed.

Once he had done this, Peter went into the kennel where, again, he broke with the conventional training method. The other instructors began the morning exercise by going up to the dogs and putting a choke chain around their necks. They then gave them a jerk so that they came to heel, then led them out of the kennel for a walk. Peter had rejected this kind of treatment completely by now and did it my way — by using food reward he got the dog to come to him then slipped a soft lead around his neck. He then took him out to walk without any jerking or pulling. If there was any of that kind of behaviour, he postponed the walk so as to get the message across that it was unacceptable.

Once outside the kennel, Peter did something else that was out of sync with the rest of the camp. He took the dog to an exercise yard where he let him off the lead and practised things like the come and the stay. In everything he was doing he was being non-aggressive, unthreatening. Every other trainer taught their dogs to sit by pushing them down. Peter knew that this was one of the main flashpoints with this dog and understood that it had to be avoided at all costs. So, again, he used food reward to encourage the dog to sit. He even spent a little time each morning doing something no other instructor there had ever done — simply playing with the dog for ten or fifteen minutes every day. Finally, he did all this without yelling and screaming like the other instructors. He did it quietly and calmly, displaying strong, firm but fair leadership throughout.

Twelve weeks after he'd left my course, Peter wrote to me. He told me that the effect had been almost immediate. Within a week the dog had calmed down hugely, with no signs of the old aggression. Within a month he was doing things that no one else had thought possible. By the time the dog had come to the end of its training programme, it had been utterly transformed. He was now a loyal, trustworthy working dog — and a great character to boot. He had passed out as top of his class. He and Peter were now starting out as a working partnership on a base in the southwest of England.

The only sad note to the story was that even when he'd been passing out, some of Peter's colleagues within the RAF were unwilling to accept what he'd achieved. While his fellow handlers had congratulated him on turning round such an unpromising dog, his instructors had simply dismissed his success as "pure luck". Peter knew it was going to take a long time to change these entrenched views. It probably won't happen in our lifetimes. But he had made a start. He had given his dog a good name — and to me that made him exceptional.

THE GLASS HALF FULL

Why great owners
are positive owners

I'm a great believer in the power of positive thinking, the idea that you should always regard the glass as half full rather than half empty.

In part, it is an extension of being open-minded, of always striving to give a dog a good name — just like Peter and his Alsatian in the previous chapter. But on a practical level it is something that can — and should — be applied on a day-to-day basis, even in the language we use. For instance, to me there are no such things as problem dogs, only challenging dogs. As far as I'm concerned, one piece of clear, positive encouragement is worth a hundred pieces of confused, unclear or, worst of all, negative communication from an owner.

The vast majority of owners with whom I work are blessed with a positive outlook. Yet every now and again one person shows me just how powerful a transforming force it can be. One such person was a lady called Andi.

Andi had a passion for the bichon frise. Many people are potty about particular breeds. There is nothing

169

wrong with this. I have a soft spot for English springer spaniels and German shepherds. Her only problem was that she couldn't stop accumulating them.

Like so many people who care about dogs, she couldn't abide the idea of abandoned dogs being destroyed. So she had set herself up to take in unwanted bichons at her home. She was known to her local rescue centre and whenever one of the breed remained unclaimed there for a period of time, it would be taken to Andi.

Her attitude was that she would take them in for as long as was needed to get them back to good health before looking to re-house them. Unfortunately, Andi's kindness had become a problem for her. She took in bichons of all ages, but quickly learned that it was difficult to find new homes for the older ones. So many of the dogs simply never left. When I met her she had no less than eight bichons, only one of whom was under twelve years old. One of them, a dog called Poppet, was seventeen.

As every dog owner knows, the cost of looking after a pet escalates sharply as they get older. So Andi's vet bills were not to be sniffed at. Yet she was not someone to give up on any of her dogs. She had a positive attitude about each animal that crossed her doorstep — her view was always: "It's not their fault they are here, now it's my job to help them lead a better life." This positive outlook was tested to the limit when she acquired a dog called Beau.

Beau arrived at Andi's home in a dreadful condition. He was nervous and rail-thin, his ribs were poking through in places. The most noticeable thing about him was the terrible condition of his coat, which kept falling out in great clumps of hair.

The bichon frise is famous for its full, dense, distinctively white coat. But Beau had hardly any coat at all. He had no fur under his body or along his right side up to his shoulder. His left side and his face only had tiny little tufts of hair. He looked moth-eaten.

As ever, Andi was prepared to do all she could to restore her newest patient to good health. She began by taking Beau back and forth to the vet. To begin with they weren't sure what he was suffering from, but after they took skin scrapings they diagnosed the problem as mange, caused by a parasite.

It was an unpleasant discovery, but Andi was relieved nevertheless. It wasn't life-threatening and at least she now knew what she was up against. She soon set about doing all she could to get rid of it. Over the course of the next six months she tried everything — shampoos, antibiotics, flea spray and a variety of different medications — but all to no avail. None of them worked.

Andi was, by nature, a hugely optimistic person. But the constant setbacks began to dent her confidence. It became a very frustrating time for her, a sensitive woman who was proud of the work she'd done in helping rescue dogs in the past. What hurt her most was the way people looked at her when she took Beau out for a walk with the rest of her pack. The looks of disapproval were unmistakable; they were saying: "What have you done to that poor dog?" It was as if it

171

was her fault he was like this. Inwardly, this began to take its toll on Andi. But, outwardly, she refused to give in.

After almost a year of false hopes and frustration her vet suggested she should give up on Beau and have him put to sleep. This was something Andi would never have contemplated. But hearing even her vet — someone she trusted and admired — suggesting they had reached the end of the road affected her deeply. People have two choices when they reach a point such this. They can either bow to the opinion of others and give in, or they can follow their own instinct, remain positive and carry on. There was never any doubt which way Andi was going to go. She told herself that Beau's condition wasn't life-threatening. He was in discomfort rather than pain, he was rundown rather than terminally ill. After giving herself a good talking to, she rediscovered her old optimism and once more looked at life as a glass half full rather than half empty. She was not going to give up. It was at this point that she heard about my method.

Andi was a bright lady and soon worked out the root of Beau's problems. His was a striking example of a dog that was way out of its depth and was being asked to do a job that was simply beyond him. Andi, like a myriad other owners, through no fault of her own, had inadvertently given Beau the idea he was responsible for her. Not only that, she was surrounded by a large pack of dogs, many of them elderly, whom Beau also regarded as below him in the pecking order. Effectively,

Beau felt burdened by the responsibility for the entire household. Was it any wonder he couldn't handle it?

As humans, we've all seen people who have been promoted to positions beyond their capabilities. You can see the terror written on their faces, and almost detect the stress levels rising within them. This is what had happened to Beau, and in his case the effects were literally written all over his body.

Andi diligently set about placing herself at the head of her pack's pecking order, thus freeing Beau from the pressure of the job. The effect was soon plain to see. Owners are often amazed at the physical effect dogs feel at having the yoke of leadership lifted off their shoulders. Often it shows first in the eyes, which become much softer. At other times it can show in the dog's demeanour. They will look more relaxed, less tensed up than they were before. They will often let out an audible sigh of relief.

In Beau's case, however, the physical evidence was even more spectacular. Within three or four weeks there was a marked improvement in Beau's condition. His coat started to grow back and soon it would have been hard to detect there had ever been anything wrong with him.

Andi wrote to me to let me know how well she'd done, and after that we stayed in contact. I was deeply impressed by her work and her general positive attitude. I genuinely admired her determination, not just with Beau, but in general towards the bichons that came into her life. She wasn't going to let any of them down.

And so it made it all the more distressing and surprising when that quality seemed to fail her. It was about two years later that she sent me a letter bringing me up to date on the latest unwelcome development in Beau's story. His life had been transformed since she'd applied my method. Beau had been a happy, carefree member of her pack. But then she took him to the vet for a routine jab. The vet noticed some problems and had run blood and tissue tests. A few days later, he called Andi in to break the bad news that Beau had cancer.

The cancer was at an advanced stage and the vet didn't see the point in performing surgery. Beau would live for a while yet and it was best, in his opinion, if he saw out those last months in peace with Andi. Naturally, the news hit Andi hard. Beau was now fourteen and in the twilight of his life anyway, but having been through so much with him it really upset her to think of losing him.

Within a week of the vet diagnosing the cancer, Andi noticed Beau's coat had begun falling out again. She rang the vet up and he assured her there could be no connection. Once more she was baffled as to what was happening. But by thinking positively and logically she soon reasoned it out.

She called me one evening to explain what had happened. "I couldn't understand it at first, but then I realised I was coming across to Beau as this emotional wreck," she told me. "What sort of a leader was that?"

It had been Andi's positive attitude that had earned Beau the extra two years they had had together. But now she had become so stressed and upset about Beau's illness that he had picked up on it.

It didn't take her long to pull herself together. She knew she could no longer deny the inevitable. The glass was — at last — becoming empty. Yet she realised that she had to apply the same mentality during the last weeks they had together as well.

Immediately she began treating him exactly as she had before, playing and walking with him as if he was another member of her pack, showing him no sign of being more worried about him than she was about any of her other dogs.

Beau lived for many more months before finally he began to suffer and he was put to sleep. As she mourned his passing, Andi could take enormous solace from the way she had behaved. She'd had her moments of hesitancy, as we all do, but by remaining focused and positive she'd given Beau a longer, happier life than he would ordinarily have been able to enjoy.

I do have a tendency to get emotionally involved with dogs and owners, particularly those who have shown exceptional qualities. Yet for some reason I found I was touched by Andi's story more deeply than usual. I have always believed in the power of positive thinking and I do believe that if you continue to have faith in something then — provided it is realistic — you have a chance of making it happen. Andi reaffirmed that view in the way she succeeded with Beau. But she showed me something else as well.

When Beau had been diagnosed with cancer, Andi's spirits had sagged, she had ceased to be the positive, decisive owner who had relieved him of his anxieties. Beau had picked up on that immediately and his old insecurities had returned with the same attendant side effects. It was a telling insight.

It made me realise in a way I had not before, just how sensitive our dogs are to even the slightest ebb and flow in our attitude to them. And it taught me how diligent we need to be in our relationship with our dogs. Most of all it made me see just how dangerous it is when you start to view the glass as half empty. It is something I've carried with me ever since.

SENSE AND SENSIBILITY

Why great owners never underestimate their dogs' instincts

The more I learn about dogs, the more I realise that we both overestimate and underestimate their abilities in about equal measure. On the one hand, we overestimate their intelligence by assuming they understand our vocal language and the rules that make our world tick as well as we do ourselves, when there is absolutely no reason why they should. This is why so many of our dogs are confused about their place in our world and it is why I believe so passionately in communicating through the instinctive language that forms the foundation stones of my method.

On the other hand — as stories like that of Andi and Beau illustrate only too well — we grossly underestimate things like their loyalty, responsiveness and, above all, their incredible sensitivity.

I don't think we'll ever fully understand the workings of the dog's brain or know the total extent of their capabilities. Yet, slowly but surely, we are seeing how much more sophisticated it is than had previously been suggested. We have known for a long time that their

177

power of smell and hearing is massively greater than our own. But every year, it seems, new studies emerge that indicate they have related powers that go far beyond this.

We've all seen small examples of this at home. I have lost count of the number of owners who have asked me why it is that the moment they pull a suitcase out of a cupboard their dog appears at their side, looking agitated. It is something I've experienced myself many times — indeed, I took part in an experiment once to try and explain it. We didn't come up with anything conclusive, but there is a body of evidence that suggests it may have something to do with their reaction to smell, specifically the smell of adrenaline generated in our bodies when we are under stress, emotional strain or have high blood pressure.

Smell also lies at the root of their habit of licking us when we come out of the bath or shower. I have heard many people say this is down to the fact that dogs like the taste of soap. I couldn't disagree more — it is to do with smell. Suddenly faced with someone who looks familiar but smells unfamiliar, they lick at us so as to remove the alien smell and get to the essence that they know. It is their way of checking it's really us, their owners.

The most fascinating development, to my mind, is that dogs are able to detect epileptic fits in humans — forty minutes before they happen. Research is still in its infancy, but the likeliest explanation is that epileptics display changes in their brain-wave patterns in the run-up to a fit. This in turn produces subtle changes in

178

the person's behaviour and smell which a dog can recognise. Whatever the explanation, epileptics are already beginning to keep dogs trained to detect the telltale signs of a fit in advance. Lives will, I'm sure, be saved as a result.

It is hard for many owners to accept that dogs are this perceptive. Perhaps this is not that surprising, because cases do sound a little fanciful, if not far-fetched. I'm not immune to the occasional doubts myself, yet every now and again I encounter a case which leaves me quietly in awe of the highly tuned nature of man's best friend.

One of the most striking cases I've ever encountered involved a lady called Angie. Angie lived with her husband, three children and three dogs, Clive, Sonny and Sophie, in Somerset. I came into contact with her originally when she was having problems with Sophie who was displaying all the conventional signs of a dog harbouring a mistaken sense of leadership: jumping up at strangers, pulling on the lead and barking continuously. But the problem that disturbed Angie and her family most of all was her toileting. Sophie urinated all over the house when Angie was away. It was a classic case of separation anxiety. Believing she was responsible for the family, Sophie reacted to their absence by panicking. She was getting into such a state that she was urinating everywhere.

This is a far from uncommon problem, and something I've dealt with many, many times over the years. Angie was an intelligent woman. After we spoke, she and her family had adopted my method and Sophie's problems had soon disappeared as Angie and the family asserted themselves as leaders of the pack.

It was about a year after I had last heard from them that Angie phoned me out of the blue. As she began to describe her problems, I felt myself wishing she'd called me earlier. Sophie had started urinating around the house again, but this time she'd also been defecating. Angie had tried reasserting herself as leader but it hadn't worked. They'd gone so far as to buy a cage to accommodate Sophie, and she had even been doing her toileting in there as well. This worried me enormously. Dogs are, by nature, clean animals and they don't generally soil their beds. I sensed there was something seriously wrong here.

Angie had mastered my method before, so I asked her what had changed since the previous year. Apparently, nothing had changed in the domestic setup. No one had left home. The dogs all remained healthy.

"There's nothing I can think of," she said.

I sensed it was down to something much subtler. Then, as we talked, Angie made a casual remark along the lines of "none of this is any good for my blood pressure".

"Have you always suffered with high blood pressure?" I asked her.

"No, only the last couple of months," she said.

As she said it, a light came on in my head.

"Does it coincide with Sophie's behaviour getting bad again?" I asked her.

180

For a moment there was a silence.

"That's impossible. It can't be, can it?" Angie said. "She couldn't have picked up on that? They're not that perceptive, are they?"

My answer to all three questions was "yes".

As I followed this line of questioning, it soon became clear that the two things were interrelated. I didn't pry into the reasons why Angie had begun to suffer higher blood pressure. That was none of my business. What Angie did confide, however, was that she had felt herself under more pressure to cope in recent weeks and that this had occasionally shown itself in her dealings with the dogs.

"I find it a struggle sometimes to keep my cool," she said. "But you can't tell me they're picking up on that."

"Don't underestimate them," I told her. "They are much more sensitive than you'd imagine."

My guess was that Sophie had indeed sensed Angie's weakness by smelling the additional adrenaline she was producing and had reassumed the mantle of leader in her own mind. Seeing that this had no effect on Angie, Sophie had begun to panic again — only this time even more acutely than before, hence her worse behaviour in terms of toileting.

In the hope of persuading Angie to my way of thinking, I asked her to assume for the time being that I was right and that Sophie had indeed picked up on her high blood pressure. What she needed to do was to reassert herself as leader of her pack. And the only way to do this was to replicate what would happen in the wild with a wolf pack.

In the wild, a wounded or weakened leader would do everything it could to mask its weakness. It would continue to demonstrate determined leadership at the four key moments, then remove itself from the pack for the rest of the time.

This, I knew, was going to be hard. Angie really loved her dogs and loved nothing more than to give them a cuddle. But, in the short term, she had to become a stricter, more remote and formal leader.

I got her, for instance, to adopt a policy of zero tolerance. If her dogs did something she disapproved of, she simply led them away from the situation.

"It's very hard to be positive when your nerves are jangling," she admitted to me, "but I'll give it a try."

After a couple of weeks, however, she called to tell me there had been progress.

"How are things?" I asked her.

"No worse," she said. "And that's a step in the right direction."

A couple of weeks after that, she let me know that Sophie had improved markedly. I knew she still had a long way to go but I was impressed at her open-mindedness and determination not to repeat the mistakes of the past. She had been guilty of underestimating her dogs' sensitivities once. She was not going to let it happen again. In the past, Angie had been a jolly lady. The most encouraging thing of all was that, as things improved, so did her old sense of humour.

At her most recent appointment with her doctor, Angie had explained how her dog had picked up on her high blood pressure.

182

"He gave me a look as if to say I wasn't just suffering from high blood pressure," she laughed.

Angie's experience taught me a valuable lesson. It illustrated yet another level of instinctive understanding at work within the canine world. And it reminded me — as if I needed it — never to underestimate a dog.

SEPARATE WORLDS

Why great owners
accept that dogs are different

It is a statement of the blindingly obvious, I know, but humans and canines inhabit different worlds. We may share our lives and homes together, we may even be able to communicate with each other to an extent, but ultimately we are members of different species.

Unfortunately, many people find this the hardest thing of all to accept. Because dogs show qualities that we recognise and appreciate, particularly wonderful human traits such as affection and loyalty, owners regard them in the same way as human friends. More significantly, they can also project their own values and ideas on to their dogs. The problem with this is they are then surprised when the dogs fail to behave as they would in a situation. To accept that this attitude is wrong is hard and sometimes upsetting. But it's a test that great owners are capable of passing. So it proved with Betty, an elderly dog owner who lived near me in North Lincolnshire.

★　★　★

Betty was retired and in her sixties. Dogs had always been a central part of her life. For many years she'd taken in rescue dogs. At the time I came into contact with her she had three dogs, two she'd had for many years, Ben and Chloe, and a relative newcomer, Sally.

Before Sally's arrival, Ben, Chloe and Betty had lived a very happy life together. Ben was now eleven, while Chloe was a very elderly thirteen. The arrival of Sally, who was just three, had upset the balance a little bit. Two dogs had been company but three became a little bit of a crowd.

Betty had been disappointed by the way the trio of dogs interacted when Sally first arrived in her home. Chloe and Ben had eyed her up warily. There had been a lot of growling and one or two confrontations during the first weeks. Betty had never experienced this before and couldn't understand it. She loved her dogs and really couldn't see why they didn't all love each other as well.

To her credit, Betty calmed things down pretty well. She saw there was some kind of rivalry or tension between the dogs and separated them when necessary. She put a gate up in her kitchen which allowed her to keep Sally with her, while Ben and Chloe had the run of the rest of the house. But this wasn't ideal so she contacted me for further help.

It was a situation I've come across many times before. I explained to Betty that there was a vacancy for leader within her pack and that Ben, Chloe and Sally were vying for the position. Their challenges to each other were part of the ritualistic process of deciding

185

who was top dog. They were sizing each other up at the moment, but there was every chance that it would get more violent. The solution, as ever, was that Betty needed to pick up the reins of leadership. There might still be some hierarchical tension among the three dogs — particularly between the newcomer Sally and the other two — but, with the main job gone, it would be nowhere near as bad.

Betty admitted that she found it hard to get her head around the ideas at the heart of my method, to look at life from the dog's perspective rather than her own. "I'm too old to be learning all this new stuff," she said to me once. I had every sympathy, since it was something I found with many owners, of all ages. Seeing things from a canine point of view rather than a human one is hard, and it is particularly hard for people who have spent their whole life thinking one way, as Betty had done.

But Betty was made of stern stuff. As someone who had been used to taking in damaged rescue dogs, she'd faced big challenges before. And to her great credit, she stuck at it and soon began to get results. As she began to establish herself as the real leader of the household, so Ben, Chloe and Sally became less anxious. With the position of leader no longer vacant, Sally and Ben in particular became reasonably friendly. While there was still the odd flare-up between Sally and Chloe, generally things calmed down considerably.

Life, however, has a nasty habit of biting you when you least expect it — or need it. It was about a year after I'd first talked to Betty that Chloe fell ill. She developed a growth on her side which needed an operation. It was touch and go for a while over whether she would be strong enough to survive the lengthy procedure. Chloe was already elderly and she seemed to be ageing even faster with her illness. When she came out of hospital she was very, very weak. Her stitches were going to take a good month or so to heal.

In order to keep an eye on her, Betty put a bed in the kitchen for Chloe. During the first few days of her convalescence, she spent most of her time there, fast asleep. Dogs sense weakness in each other, and if there has been a history of confrontation — as there had been here — owners have to be very careful when one member of a pack is ill. The roots of this, as ever, lie in the wolf pack. In the wild, a wolf pack cannot tolerate weakness. If they sense one member of the pack is, for whatever reason, unable to contribute they will abandon it.

Betty sensed the danger and to give Chloe a better chance of recovery she had kept the other two dogs separated from her, on the other side of the gate. Unfortunately, she wasn't careful enough. One morning, Betty stepped out of the kitchen briefly leaving the gate unlocked.

She was in the bathroom when she heard the most terrifying noise, a yelp that just cut through the air. Instinctively she knew what it must be, but it was only when she saw all three of her dogs fighting each other that she accepted it was happening.

The scene that greeted Betty was truly awful. Both Ben and Sally had attacked Chloe. They were tearing into her with a viciousness that made Betty feel physically sick. She just screamed at the top of her voice. It was fortunate that all three of her dogs were relatively small. Betty was able to intervene, grabbing Chloe and lifting her free. Even then Sally tried to bite at Chloe as she cowered in Betty's arms. Betty found herself batting Sally away with her arms.

Betty saw that the damage caused was considerable. One of the dogs had taken a gouge out of Chloe's nose and there was blood on her mouth. The only consolation was that the stitches in Chloe's side were untouched.

Nevertheless, Chloe was absolutely traumatised, and was shivering in Betty's arms. Betty headed back to the bathroom where she locked the door. She could still hear the two dogs barking behind her and it took her an age to compose herself. She then quietly bathed Chloe's wounds and laid her on the bathroom floor wrapped in a towel.

Betty later told me that she had no idea how long she'd sat there. When she'd eventually calmed down she went outside and put Sally and Ben outside in the garden. She then called me. She was in floods of tears throughout our conversation. As we talked, I listened to her go through a host of emotions. At first, she was angry at Sally.

"Everything was OK until she turned up," she said. "She's a hateful dog."

I knew it was the emotion of the moment rather than her real feelings that were making her say this. "It's not Sally's fault," I reassured Betty. "It's sad, I know, but it's the way any dog would have behaved in that situation."

Next, she blamed herself. "It's my fault, I shouldn't have brought her here," she said. "If I'd left her in the centre this wouldn't have happened."

"You didn't know Chloe was going to get ill, how can it be your fault?" I asked.

Ultimately, however, Betty's main feeling was one of confusion. She loved her dogs and simply didn't understand why they didn't love each other. "I love all of them the same, why can't they feel the same way?" she kept saying to me. "Why do they have to fight?"

The truth is that dogs don't feel the same way. They are governed by their instincts, their reactions are hard-wired into them. And this is something that we will never be able to breed or train out of them. As I've said many times: "You can take the dog out of the wolf pack, but you can't take the wolf pack out of the dog." Ben and Sally had sensed weakness within their own pack and had acted on it.

Betty really didn't want to believe this. "Surely not . . ." she said repeatedly.

"I'm afraid so," I kept replying.

It was a difficult thing to accept. Betty found it really hard to believe that dogs don't see the world as we do.

She remained badly shaken for days afterwards. She almost jumped out of her skin every time she heard a sound that was slightly unusual. Betty knew that she had to do something to avoid a repeat of the scenes she had witnessed in the kitchen. So, reluctantly and with a heavy heart, she decided that her pack had to be segregated for their own safety.

It was something I understood fully. I told Betty about the awful experience I'd had myself when I'd lost two of my most cherished dogs, Sasha and Barmie, in the space of a terrible two days, a year or so earlier. Their loss had been such a blow it had left me reeling and I had briefly forgotten to adhere to my method. My remaining dogs had reacted immediately. Sasha had been the most dominant canine in the pack of seven dogs and her absence had immediately changed the dynamic. By seemingly relinquishing my role as overall leader, I'd only added to the sense that the job was now vacant. Four of my six dogs had attacked each other with a violence that had shocked me.

The long-term impact of the fight had been immense. Because the dynamic of the pack was also being affected by my increased absence through my work, I, too, had had to live in the real world and make some tough choices. For a while, I'd also had to separate the warring elements within my own pack. It had been a tough thing to do.

"If they'd been humans they'd have allowed some time for grieving, they'd have made allowances for my lack of leadership," I told Betty. "But they're not humans, they're canines."

Betty accepted that she had to take similar action. From then on Chloe was kept apart from the other two. Occasionally she would let her old playmate Ben spend time with her, under Betty's watchful eye, of course.

But Sally and Chloe were never allowed to be close to each other.

"That's just the way it's got to be," Betty said to me once. "It's like it is with your children, you can't choose their friends for them. You've got to live with their choices. The other two don't get on with Chloe any more, and I've got to live with that." I was rather touched by the analogy, I must admit. It has stayed with me ever since.

As it happened, Chloe's time was drawing to a close. Some nine months after her operation she slipped away. Betty was mortified. Chloe had been a loyal friend for the best part of ten years. Yet, much as she would have liked to do, she didn't replace her. She herself was getting older and she didn't feel she had what was needed to take on another rescue dog. She had already proved it to me, but even in that act Betty underlined that she was an owner from whom we can all learn something.

LETTING GO

The importance of knowing when to say goodbye

It is the moment every dog lover dreads — and the one we know we cannot escape. As owners like Betty will readily confirm, losing our dogs is a terribly hard thing to go through. But there's a right way to go about it, and a wrong one.

In the course of my life, I have had to say goodbye to a long line of dogs. And, inevitably, I will have to see many more leave this life. It hasn't got any easier to bear the losses, but at least I have learned to understand the importance of letting go.

I am often asked about coping with this grievous time. How should it be handled? What coping mechanisms should we use? The answer, of course, is that the circumstances are going to be different for each of us. It is hard to generalise. But if pressed, I recall as an example my own daughter Ellie and her loss of her one and only dog, Susie, in the 1980s. The way she coped was an inspiration to me — and should be to everyone when they come to face that dreadful day.

★ ★ ★

Ellie had been given her dog Susie for her seventh birthday. She'd been asking for one for a long time before that, but I'd put it off until I felt she was a reasonably responsible age. It would be her responsibility to look after the dog, to feed it, walk it and groom it, so I wanted to be sure she understood the meaning of the commitment. She did, becoming a devoted friend instantly.

I didn't grasp it at first, but it turned out Susie filled a huge emotional need in Ellie's life. Shortly before getting Susie, Ellie had lost a close schoolfriend, a girl called Susie Clarkson. Susie had died of leukaemia, aged just six. Her loss devastated everyone at her school and in the local community.

Ellie had been deeply upset by this — she couldn't understand it. She'd become very quiet and withdrawn and hadn't played so much. Susie arrived in her life at just the right time. In no way did we get a dog to replace her friend in some way. It was something we planned long before events took such a terrible turn. But the effect on Ellie was immediate. When we asked her what she was going to call the dog she looked at us as if we were a bit dim.

"Susie, of course."

She had spoken to our friend Jim Moss about its importance.

One day I met Jim out walking with his dog Ben. He told me he'd been chatting to Ellie who'd said something that had affected him deeply. "She said: 'I haven't got the real Susie any more, so this Susie's my friend now'," Jim told me.

193

Susie and Ellie were inseparable throughout her childhood. When she was nine, my marriage to her father broke up. The divorce was a terribly difficult time for us all. Again Ellie retreated into a shell a little, spending all her time behind the closed door of her bedroom. But Susie was always there with her, curling up at the bottom of her bed while she did her homework and sleeping close by every night.

My son Tony's dog, Sandy, performed a similar role for him.

When she reached eighteen, however, it was time for Ellie and Susie to be separated. Ellie went off to university in Swansea and Susie stayed with me and my other dogs. It felt odd to see her without her constant companion. Susie's spirits sagged a little. Whenever Ellie came home for her holidays, she was transformed — as was Ellie, who said she found it hard to go away without her. There were tears each time she left to go back to university.

Every time she telephoned home, her first words were: "Hi, Mum, how's Susie?"

By the time Ellie was approaching the end of her first year, the answer to that question was "not too good". The truth was that Susie was getting old and very frail. Since Ellie had left, she'd grown weak and listless and wasn't eating well. She was unsteady on her feet too and had had a couple of accidents. I'd sensed she might not have much longer with us, but hadn't said as much to Ellie for fear of upsetting her. I knew that she'd see it for herself when she came home.

When she arrived back for her summer holiday, Susie was pleased to see her, but it was obvious the dog lacked the energy of old. Ellie didn't say much, but she didn't need to. It was while we were out walking all the dogs in the fields of a friend Jane's farm one Saturday morning that things came to a head. Somehow Susie stumbled and fell into a ditch. The first I knew of it was when I heard this sickening, piercing yelp of pain. Fortunately, she hadn't done any serious physical damage to herself, but as Ellie picked her out it was clear she was deeply distressed. I knew that it would be unfair to let her go on growing weaker every day. It wasn't my decision to make, however.

I remember Ellie just sitting there hugging Susie close to her. After a while, I sat down with her, wrapping my arms around her and consoling her.

"What do we do, Mum? I don't know what to do," she said.

"I think it's time to let her go," I said. "But she's your dog, it's up to you."

Ellie sat there, the tears rolling down her cheek, poor Susie shivering in her arms. Ellie stroked her and whispered to her quietly, but nothing she could do could ease her suffering.

I have no idea how long we sat there. Eventually, Ellie composed herself and said, "Let's ring the vet, we should do it."

We carried Susie into Jane's house. She rang the vet for us but was horrified when he said he couldn't see us until Monday morning.

Jane was not a woman to mince her words. "Do you realise how much courage it's taken this young girl to make this decision?" she shouted at the vet.

Needless to say, she never used him again.

Fortunately, there was another vet in the area, a young Australian. He told us to come straight over.

He was a marvellous vet, with a really lovely manner. "Hello, Susie," he said as he took her from Ellie. He was ever so gentle with her. I had been unsure whether Ellie would want to be there at the end. But when I suggested she might not she gave me a look of bewilderment, as if to say, "What on earth are you talking about?" She sat with Susie, stroking her and whispering her goodbyes as the vet administered the injection. Only when Susie slipped away were there tears. She remained strong for her friend until then.

Back at home, Ellie, Jane and I prepared a small grave in the garden.

No parent likes to see their child upset. It broke my heart to see the suffering she was going through. I'd lost a few dogs in my life and understood the pain she was feeling. Yet I was filled with admiration for the way she had dealt with the situation. I don't think I had been as strong when I'd gone through the same thing.

What struck me that day was how instinctively right Ellie had been in everything she did. I had never really analysed my own behaviour in saying goodbye to a dog. She made me think about what was right in the circumstances more deeply than I had done before. From then on, I used her example as a yardstick both for myself and in guiding others to make the difficult decision to let go.

At one point Ellie said to me, "I can't remember life before Susie." When I sat and thought about it, I realised that she'd had her for twelve years, two-thirds of her life. Yet despite the depth of that relationship Ellie had known instinctively that to have prolonged Susie's suffering would have been a betrayal of that lifelong friendship. And Ellie wasn't someone to betray the best friend she'd ever had. That was the first thing she taught me that day.

The second was that, much as it hurt her, Ellie did the kindest, most humane thing — and she did it as fast as she could. It is something I always advise people to do when they know the end has come — do it humanely and swiftly. It is the least you owe your dog.

The third thing, and perhaps most profound thing she taught me that day was the importance of sharing that moment with your dog. In thinking about our own departure from this life, I'm sure we would all like to think of ourselves surrounded by the faces we most love. Why should we deny our dogs that privilege? To my mind, it is the least we can do to honour and thank them for the pleasure and companionship they have provided. This is something I have made a rule in my life — and advocate powerfully to all owners to whom I speak about this difficult area.

Of course, we all want our dogs to live for ever and will all do whatever we can to prolong their lives medically. But there comes a time when that decision has to be made. Ellie taught me that the manner in

which those final hours are treated can say as much —
if not more — about an owner as the way they behave
during the dog's entire lifetime.

Ellie has never owned another dog. Having seen the
way she handled Susie's passing, in my eyes she
remains a great owner nevertheless.

IN SICKNESS AND IN HEALTH

When their dogs grow weak, great owners grow strong

It's easy to be a good friend to your dog when it's at its best. Life becomes a lot harder when illness strikes, and the way owners deal with their dogs in these circumstances is — to my mind — one of the acid tests of their abilities.

In the first place, it can be a crippling financial burden. I know from experience that vets' bills can bring tears to the eyes. But even more testing is the emotional strain. Caring for a patient that cannot tell you exactly how it is feeling and that often deals with its pain in inexplicable ways is not easy.

For some people it can all prove too much. Weaker owners often buckle under the pressure and either give their ailing dogs to a sanctuary or even have them put down when there is no real need to do so.

However, some owners seem to thrive on the challenge that faces them in these difficult circumstances. Two ladies in particular, Jeannette and Yvonne, were

199

instrumental in teaching me how really great owners grow stronger as their dogs grow weaker.

Jeannette lived in Brighton with her large Irish wolfhound Murphy. Jeannette had bought Murphy when he was eight weeks old. Within a short time of his arrival, he had begun showing signs of a pronounced limp. At first, she thought little of it, but it had soon become bad enough for her to seek medical attention. She was told that it might be caused by calcification in his joints, particularly the "elbow" joint at the top of the legs. This is something that is common to big breeds when they are growing fast. It is a painful, debilitating condition and can have severe consequences. Dogs can become severely disabled — or worse.

It is something that can clear up as dogs get older, but in Murphy's case it had only become more severe. Things were made no easier by the fact that Murphy's behaviour was bad as well. He would run around the house and bark and jump up at people. Even when he was a one-year-old he was a giant of a dog so it was no joke to have him imposing himself on anyone. What was really disturbing about this was that the more excited he became, the more exaggerated and painful-looking the limp became. Murphy was in a vicious circle that was spiralling downhill fast. His health wasn't helping his agitated behaviour, and his agitated behaviour was having a detrimental effect on his health.

As usual, people had come forward with all sorts of unhelpful advice, and Jeannette had also been back and forth to the vet in the previous months. One had very unhelpfully suggested the problem was that Murphy had "only two brain cells — and neither of them works". Unsurprisingly, Jeannette had switched vet. She was now being told that Murphy needed an operation to fix his joints. But if it didn't work, there were two possible scenarios. If the operation wasn't successful the vet would have no option but to amputate the affected leg. Many dogs cope with amputation well. But the vet's fear was that — because of his size and, significantly, his behaviour — Murphy would not. They were genuinely worried that if this was the case, the downward spiral would continue. The second, and worst-case, scenario was that Jeannette would have to face putting him down, something no one wanted.

Murphy's best chance of coming through the operation was to wait another six months or so, until he was fully grown, around the age of two. But, if he carried on the way he was, there was no way he could wait that long, such was the deterioration in his mobility. The only way Murphy's joints were going to last long enough was if he calmed down and didn't put so much pressure on them all the time.

When Jeannette turned to me for help, her opening words were, "I'm at my wits' end." And when I met Murphy for the first time, I had every sympathy with her. Poor old Murphy really was his own worst enemy. The moment I walked into the house he bounded at me in his exuberant way. I just gave him the cold shoulder, as I always do in such cases, planting the first seed of doubt in his mind about his status in comparison to me. When he tried to jump up a second time, so as to impose his authority, I held his collar and kept him down and at a distance from me. "He's just hyperactive like this all the time," Jeannette explained apologetically.

If there's one word that I'd like to see banned from usage in connection with dogs it is "hyperactive". It has become one of those convenience words that everyone reaches for without thinking. Jeannette had made this mistake too.

"Your dog is not hyperactive, it's just extremely muddled up," I told her. I went on to explain what I thought was wrong, that he was under the mistaken impression he was leader of their "pack" and was therefore responsible for her. Jeannette's behaviour around him was inadvertently only reinforcing this belief.

I won't deny it was hard work calming Murphy down. Within a few minutes of my taking him by the collar and keeping him at a distance, he'd given up. He just flopped theatrically to the floor — as if he'd collapsed. I held him there for a second with the collar. I knew that wasn't going to be the end of it — far from it. No sooner had I let go of the collar, than he bounded up again. So I went through the process again — and he was soon on the floor again. I repeated this about six times before he stopped jumping up and remained lying on the carpet. No sooner had I done this than Jeannette's daughter, Toni, popped in. Immediately, the good work of earlier was undone and he was bounding at her.

This time I had to hold him by the collar for a good minute before he calmed down. At one point I sat down on a chair but he bounded up with such power that he dragged me off on to my knees. By the time I left Jeannette later that day I had laid what I thought were promising foundations for her future behaviour towards Murphy. She understood that it wasn't Murphy's fault and that the key now was to remain calm and consistent. But I could see she was going to have a hard task.

One thing Jeannette didn't lack was determination. She knew she had to break this vicious circle if she was to have a chance of saving Murphy from losing his leg and she was prepared to put in the work. She called me on an almost daily basis for guidance. If Jeanette was short of anything, it was confidence and she would often say things like: "He'll do it for you, but not for me." On other occasions, she'd call me in tears because of some setback.

Jeannette made good progress in defusing moments of "danger" by simply saying "thank you" to Murphy when he reacted to them. He'd begun to understand that Jeannette was the leader and this was enough for him to calm down when visitors arrived. But one morning, a week or so into the process, the postman had come to the door and knocked particularly loudly. Despite Jeannette's efforts to thank him, Murphy propelled himself at the glass door, shattering the glass with the force of the head butt he delivered.

For the future I suggested Jeannette keep Murphy on a lead during the times of day when she might expect visitors. Again, she was adamant that she was going to make Murphy's life better and so she went along with this. Throughout this time, my job was to keep her focused on the good things she'd achieved — and soon there were plenty of them. About a month after I first visited her, Jeannette rang me with some good news.

"I really think I've made the breakthrough. He's generally much calmer now and his limp is hardly noticeable sometimes," she said.

I got some even better news a few weeks after that when she took Murphy back to the vet. The strain on his joints had obviously been reduced over the previous weeks. The vet told Jeannette the operation could now be put back safely by at least six months, giving it a much better chance of success. Things carried on in this vein right until the time finally came for Murphy to go into hospital.

By that time Murphy was already twenty months old. The vet fixed plates onto his joints and, thankfully, Murphy suffered no adverse reaction. Back home he was even able to walk around in a plaster cast without any return to the manic behaviour of the past. It took a little time for the vet to be sure things were OK, but eventually Jeannette heard that the procedure had been a complete success. Murphy's growing was all but over by then. He was never going to be completely free of his difficulties, but he could certainly look forward to a much more mobile and happy life.

In lesser hands, I dread to think what might have happened to Murphy. But fate had dealt him a winning hand, and he had ended up with an exceptional owner.

Thanks to her perseverance and strength, his hobbling days were over.

It's rare that one comes across owners of this calibre, but I've been lucky enough to encounter a few. Not long after I'd met Jeannette, another owner of a troubled dog, Yvonne, provided me with a further, revelatory moment.

Yvonne bred King Charles spaniels, cavaliers or "cavvies" as they are popularly known, specialising in a particularly striking strain of the breed, Blenheims, with a beautiful red and white colouring.

A year or so before I met her, one of her dogs, Sophie, produced a litter of four puppies: two boys and two girls. At first they looked like a perfectly normal, healthy litter. They just lay there like little suckling machines. But as the weeks wore on, Yvonne began to notice that the biggest dog in the litter, one of the boys, Elliott, yelped a lot, as if he was in pain. He also seemed a lot clumsier than the other three. Concerned by this, she took him to her vet.

By now Elliott was five or six weeks old. The vet didn't take long to reach a verdict.

"I'm afraid he's totally blind," he told Yvonne. It turned out that Elliott couldn't even distinguish between light and dark, that's how severe his disability was.

The vet knew this presented Yvonne with a real dilemma.

"It's up to you. We would not advocate putting him down, but it will be a tough life for you and him," he said.

Yvonne was, naturally, very upset. Back home she sat down with her husband and children, asking each of them what they felt should be done with Elliott. The decision was unanimous. They all loved him to pieces and couldn't bear the thought of having him put down. It was decided they'd keep him — regardless of his disability and the problems this might bring.

The family did all they could to make the house an environment in which Elliott could feel safe and secure. They put up special gates to ensure he couldn't get out of the house onto the road outside. They agreed that the furniture should always be kept in precisely the same place so that Elliott could learn to negotiate his way around the house without injuring himself. Even so, as the vet predicted, life was extremely difficult.

The main problem was that Elliott was very demonstrative, and everything he did was over the top. He would charge around like a bull at a gate, bumping into things regularly. He would also growl at the other puppies and even his own mother sometimes. Yvonne and the family weren't immune from the odd snarl, and even a snap if they tried to touch him when he was agitated.

Elliott was at his worst at mealtimes. The moment he smelled food he would barrel his way to the kitchen, knocking aside everyone and everything that stood between him and the bowl. He would instantly nip at anyone who came near him when he was eating, something he did as if his life depended upon it.

The family could cope with the blindness, but they found this manic behaviour harder to handle,

206

particularly as it was completely at odds with that of his mother Sophie. They were also concerned because Elliott's behaviour was having a knock-on effect on the rest of the dogs. Whenever Yvonne called one dog now, they'd all come charging at her, a bundle of overexcited energy, each of them.

Yvonne had taken on the responsibility of looking after Elliott and she was determined to help him. She could tell that he was deeply unhappy. Cavaliers have a lovely expression on their faces that sometimes looks as if they are almost smiling, but Elliott tended to walk with his head down and wearing a hangdog expression, almost as if he was frowning. Yvonne guessed all this was a reaction to his blindness. Instinctively, Elliott must have known there was something wrong with him. Was there some way she could ease that anxiety, make him a happier dog? It was at this point that she called me in.

It was a new experience for me. I had not worked with a blind dog before and knew it would test me. But I also knew that the pack dynamics weren't going to be any different just because there was a member with an impairment. In planning the approach to take, I made a decision that I had, in effect, to ignore Elliott's blindness. I had to bring some kind of harmony to the pack and make him feel as if he was an ordinary member of it.

I was pretty sure I would find owners who were making the usual mistakes. Sure enough, Yvonne was committing the sorts of well-intentioned errors I've seen in countless houses. For instance, she was leaving

207

food down permanently for Elliott. I could understand her thinking here — he was blind and might not be able to let her know he was hungry sometimes. But I explained to her the effect it had on him and on the other dogs who also fed from the bowl. This just reinforced the idea that the role of food provider — and therefore leader — was theirs rather than hers. She was also making a great fuss of the dogs when she came in through the front door, again something that is anathema to a canine leader, who would walk in and ignore its subordinates so as to re-establish itself as top dog. These two elements were problems that were easily fixed, although initially Yvonne was shocked to discover that, rather than being her babies, her puppies actually regarded themselves as being responsible for her and the rest of the family.

After analysing the situation more fully, it became clear to me that the main priority in this household was to calm things down. Yvonne had told me how agitated Elliott became and I had seen for myself the way all the dogs charged at her whenever she called one of them. I saw that Elliott needed the place to be calm and quiet so that he could properly focus on the sound of his owner's voice, not only what it was asking him to do, but also the direction from which it was coming so that he could head towards it as directed. This seemed to me the real flashpoint in the house so I decided to start here.

We worked on reuniting the pack after a separation. The key was to get each of the dogs — not just Elliott — to recognise the specific sound of its own name. I began this process by calling out for one dog, letting that dog through, then gently blocking and deflecting the rest. We would repeat this until the dogs learned whether to approach or not depending on the name called out. As we did this, I wasn't in the least surprised to see that the quickest to latch on was Elliott. Invariably, when one dog goes wrong within a pack it is the smartest of them, the one that is asking the most questions about its situation. But slowly the message began to get through to his siblings as well.

Within half an hour, the rest of the puppies had got the picture too and the whole pack had calmed down considerably. I assured Yvonne that provided she made the changes I wanted and adhered to the other key elements of my method, Elliott and the rest of the dogs would be a much easier proposition.

It is very easy for me to go into a home and straighten things out in a short time. I have had years of experience at it, and understand the principles at work. It is far harder for an owner to achieve the same effect, especially when they need to make huge adjustments to their life. Yvonne was the sort of woman who filled me with confidence. I felt sure she'd get it right — and she did.

Cases like this make my job a rewarding, life-affirming experience. Of course, the satisfaction I get from helping ease a difficult situation is huge. But it is much more than simply leaving a happy household behind as I head home. On this occasion, I'd come away having learned as much — if not more — than the owners I had been asked to help. I'd never had to work with a blind dog before and it had helped me develop my ideas still further.

Yet again, the real lesson was the lengths that people are prepared to go to ensure their dogs lead a happy and rewarding life. Long after I'd left, Yvonne and her family were still doing whatever it took to make Elliott comfortable.

Of course, they could not ignore the fact that Elliott was completely blind. When Yvonne wanted to rearrange the furniture in the living room, for instance, she prepared Elliott for it by adding cardboard boxes to the ends of the pieces that were going to be moved. The idea was that if he was running around, as he often did, he would begin by bumping into these soft obstacles and adjust his route around the house before much heavier and potentially painful objects were put in their place.

But the greatest sacrifice came when Yvonne's husband was offered a new job in Sheffield. All families make their calculations at times like these and Yvonne's was no different. They lived in a lovely, quiet country setting and were very happy there. More to the point their dogs — and Elliott in particular — were content there too. They were seriously concerned that a noisier, city environment might disorientate and upset Elliott. So eventually — as a family — they decided to pass on the job offer.

As time went by, I remained in contact with them and was pleased to hear that Elliott had grown into a contented and relatively trouble-free little dog. His blindness won't affect his life expectancy, of course. With owners like Yvonne and her family, I'm sure he'll live to a ripe old age. They should be an inspiration to us all.

THROUGH THICK AND THIN

How great owners show strength for their dog's sake

For many people, dogs are a great escape, a wonderful diversion from the sometimes unhappy realities of life. There are times when real life comes crashing down on us all. The ripples affect everyone close to us — our dogs included — and the manner in which we deal with such times of crisis says much about our qualities as owners. In recent years, I have been fortunate enough to meet people who have taught me much about how we can all rise to meet the challenges of such situations.

When Michael and Patricia first approached me about buying Murphy, one of a litter of German shepherd pups born to my dog Sasha, I have to confess I was a little unsure of them. Michael contacted me initially by telephone. During our conversation, he explained that Patricia was confined to a wheelchair and that he was her full-time carer.

This worried me. Ever since my early days as a breeder and my experiences with Evelyn and John

212

Needham, I had applied strict criteria to anyone buying a dog from me. I wouldn't, for instance, let one of my dogs go to a family where everyone was out at work all day. There had to be someone available to spend time with the dog. When I learned of Michael and Patricia's circumstances, I had serious doubts that they could provide the care and attention a dog needed. Given the workload Michael faced, I couldn't see how he would have the spare time to walk him, let alone feed and play with a dog as energetic as Murphy.

My concerns eased immediately when I met them. Patricia was paralysed, she spoke very slowly and only had the use of her left hand. Michael had been looking after her for six months or so and was clearly finding it a strain. It was clear also that, for Michael in particular, Murphy would be a lifeline. As we chatted, he explained that he wanted a dog to get him out of the house on daily walks. "It'll be so good for me," he said.

As was often the case, it was my dogs who gave me the strongest indication about the suitability of their aspirant owners. I've seen members of my pack back away from potential owners in the past. Each time it has happened, I've listened to them and decided against giving a dog to that person. But on this occasion, I saw the opposite reaction. Soon after Patricia had arrived in the house, my German shepherd Sasha moved over to the left side of her wheelchair. Once in position, she placed her head under Patricia's left arm so that she could touch it. It was typical of her. Not only did she feel safe with Patricia, she somehow sensed her vulnerability.

213

Within an hour or so of meeting Patricia and Michael, my mind was put at rest. They were going to provide him with all he needed, and they were going to be good, responsible, loving owners. They asked me whether I wanted to check their house out before handing over Murphy. I didn't feel I needed to; instead I offered to deliver the dog to them and, when I did so, it only underlined my feeling that everything was going to be fine. The house was set up to meet all Patricia's needs. But they had also prepared for Murphy's arrival with a big new bed, a cosy blanket and a collection of toys.

As they left, I said what I always say to people who take one of my dogs. "If there's any problem, you can bring the dog back to me." Michael's response was heartfelt, but typical. "This boy's going to change my life, he's not going anywhere."

Sure enough, Michael's life was transformed by Murphy. He got him out of the house every day and they walked miles together. We stayed in touch and talked often on the phone. Michael even sent me a photograph of the two of them out walking. From the expressions on their faces, it was hard to tell who was having the better time — Michael or Murphy.

Eight months after Murphy left, I received a phone call from one of the nurses looking after Patricia. Her voice was grave. "I understand you're the breeder of Murphy," she said. I have to confess, my immediate instinct was to assume that Patricia had taken a turn for the worse. I was stunned when I learned it was John.

"I'm afraid John died of a heart attack this morning," the nurse told me. "Things are very difficult here at the moment as I'm sure you'll appreciate. Someone needs to take care of the dog right away."

She didn't need to say any more. I headed straight over.

Patricia was obviously distressed, as was her daughter who had travelled to her mother's side that morning. Murphy, too, was clearly disoriented by all the activity. He was anxious, pacing around, his eyes darting across the room restlessly. Patricia wasn't happy to see me. She'd clearly understood the implication of my being there and let me know it. "Please don't take my dog," she asked me.

It was clearly an inappropriate environment for Murphy. The family had a lot to deal with in the coming days. "I've got to for now," I told Patricia. I explained to her daughter that we'd talk again when things had calmed down a little. I felt awful driving away with Murphy, but at the same time I was sure I'd done the right thing. There wasn't an alternative.

After the funeral, Patricia rang me. She sounded weak but was determined to talk to me about Murphy. I was hoping she was going to make the right decision, but understood when she said she hadn't been able to make up her mind about him. I reassured her that he was well and told her to take her time.

It was another two weeks before I heard from her again. This time she asked me to her house to see her. I arrived to find she had a full-time helper and was getting on with her life. I sat down with her over a cup of tea and listened to what she had to say.

"I've got to be practical about this, haven't I?" she said.

I nodded.

"I'm not going to be able to keep him, am I?"

This time I shook my head slowly. "No, I don't think so, Patricia," I said, squeezing her hand.

There were tears rolling down her face.

"John loved him so much, he was such a joy to us both," she said.

I reassured her that I'd find Murphy another good, loving home.

When I found him a home with another family, I rang Patricia to let her know. The family were ever so good to her, regularly sending her photographs of Murphy and letting her know how he was getting on.

It was a very brave thing Patricia did. In her heart, I know, she needed company perhaps more than she had ever needed companionship before. Yet she was also realistic enough to know she couldn't care for Murphy properly. She did the right thing, and that's something for which I'll always admire her.

Patricia's story is a powerful one, but so too is that of Colin, who took another of my German shepherd puppies, Simba, a few years earlier.

With his wife, Mary, Colin approached me about getting Simba in the mid-1990s. They met the criteria for potential owners with ease. It was their first

German shepherd so even before meeting me they had researched the breed thoroughly, reading up on things like hip displacia and diet. I had no fears about Simba being left alone either. Colin worked shifts so had a lot of spare time during the day.

"We'll be outside every day, the colder the better," Colin told me.

To no one's surprise they turned out to be smashing owners. Colin and Mary were so good with Simba that eighteen months later they had another shepherd pup from me, Max.

Over the months and years we became quite good friends. So it was with a heavy heart that I heard Colin and Mary had separated. I had been through a marital break-up myself and I knew how hard it is. Mary left with the children. She also took Max, while Colin kept Simba. It was typical of them that they called me to ask whether this was all right. "As long as you can cope," I told them both.

While Mary and the children settled into a new flat, Colin struggled and his life took a turn for the worst. He was diagnosed with cancer of the aorta. It was a vigorous form of the disease and he was only given a short time to live. It never ceases to amaze me where people get the strength from at times like these, but as he began his fight with the disease and underwent radiotherapy, Colin also got on with the business of putting his affairs in order.

His family weren't quite so collected, however, and they took it out on Mary whom they blamed for Colin's illness. She found herself pushed away. She was told she was not welcome at Colin's bedside. Only the children were allowed to see him. This was a difficult thing for Mary to deal with and became doubly so when Colin was admitted to hospital.

Colin went downhill fast and died, leaving everyone who had known him devastated. The funeral was a dignified affair, with none of the tensions to the fore. But in the days immediately afterwards, Simba became the subject of something of a battle royal within the family.

Colin had been deeply concerned about Simba, and in particular he was concerned about who would look after him when he went into hospital. Colin was one of three brothers and one of his siblings, Nicholas, had always taken an interest in Simba. Everyone knew he was completely unsuitable as an owner — he used to tease the dog so much the children would hide Simba away whenever they saw him arriving. Colin was adamant that he didn't want Nicholas looking after Simba and had made arrangements for him to be put into a good local kennels while he was in hospital. In the days after the funeral, Nicholas immediately laid claim to Simba. "I'm having that dog," he told the families.

As the person who had been closest to Simba, Mary was appalled by this. She made it clear that she was opposed to Nicholas becoming Simba's owner. She had a word with the owner of the kennels who in turn told Nicholas she wasn't going to give the dog to anyone until she was given legal authority to do so.

218

So it was, a short time later, that the family gathered at Colin's solicitors for the reading of his will. Colin had spent the final weeks of his life ensuring that everything was covered. To no one's surprise, his children had been his priority and they were the main benefactors of the will. For Nicholas and other family members, the big shock was that Simba, too, had been taken into account. Any hopes Nicholas — or anyone else in the family — might have had of acquiring him were dashed in one sentence. "My dog Simba will be taken back to his breeder, Jan Fennell," Colin had written.

When Mary rang me up to tell me, I was overwhelmed. As sick as he was, as consumed by emotion and fear as he must have been, Colin had put the future of his dog on a par with that of his children. He had taken a hard, considered look at the situation and concluded that the idea of leaving his dog to his brother — or indeed anyone unsuitable — was simply unacceptable.

Soon afterwards, I took a copy of the will along to the kennels and brought Simba home. Within a month or so, I found him a super new home in Yorkshire, where he still lives happily. To me Colin's selfless courage and wisdom was something remarkable. And the memory of it has stayed with me.

Until then, I hadn't realised how far we all need to go in considering our dog's welfare. It made me see that we are all guilty at times of shutting out the stark realities of life. And it made me understand that by doing so we risk failing to do the one thing we work so hard for in life — caring for and providing for the ones we love.

Colin made me realise that we are all flesh and blood and, just as we provide for our families, so too we should think of what will happen to our dogs if, heaven forbid, something unexpected happens. My dogs are well cared for, I know, but in the wake of Colin leaving us, I found myself asking what would happen to them if I wasn't there. All great owners will do the same.

REAPING THE REWARDS

Why you only get out
what you put in

You only get out what you put in. I don't know who first came up with this expression, but it is so true. And it applies as much to our relationships with dogs as it does to every other aspect of life.

It is something I am constantly reminded of when I meet owners. Almost always, those who have enjoyed the most rewarding relationships with dogs have been those who were prepared to go that extra mile for them. Few owners I have encountered illustrate this better than Steve, a divorcee, living alone near Great Yarmouth, in Norfolk.

Steve had led a full and exciting life. He worked as a deep-sea diver, a job that had taken him all over the world, including spells living and working in America and Australia. In the years since his marriage broke up, he had settled down to a quieter life in the Norfolk countryside. He was still close to his grown-up children who visited him there.

Steve hadn't planned to have a dog, it was the last thing on his mind. But then one day he was approached by two friends, Jane and Sarah, who ran a local dog kennels. Out of the blue, they asked him whether he'd be able to dig them out of a corner by looking after a rescue dog they had in their care, an English springer spaniel called Pepe. They were temporarily short of space and needed someone to watch over her briefly.

"It would only be a couple of days," they reassured Steve.

Steve's family had had dogs when he was growing up, but as an adult he'd never owned one. Talk about being thrown in at the deep end: it turned out that Pepe wasn't just a rescue dog, she was also suffering from diabetes.

Just as in humans, diabetes is a relatively common ailment in dogs. And as with humans, it's a condition that needs careful monitoring. Jane and Sarah explained that Pepe needed twice-daily injections of insulin, one at 8.00 in the morning and another at 4.30 in the afternoon. She also needed three feeds a day, each time made up of a specially designed diet. They knew it was asking a lot and offered to come round to administer the treatment.

Steve was understandably apprehensive, but agreed to help his friends out. "I'll do my best," he said. He was pleasantly surprised when Pepe arrived the following day. She was a lovely, liver and white four-year-old bitch. No sooner had she arrived than she settled down under the computer desk where Steve spent most of his working day.

222

That afternoon, Jane arrived to administer the 4.30 injection. Steve asked to be shown how to do it. He also asked what would be needed if Pepe had an episode, as diabetics often did. "Oh, you shouldn't have to worry about that," said Jane. "And if she's not right, just give us a call, we'll be right round."

Perhaps because safety issues were so important in his line of work, Steve was adamant. "Just in case, I'd like to know," said Steve.

"Honey and water," said Jane. "But mostly honey."

Steve took Pepe out for a walk late that afternoon. It was high summer and his village was surrounded by stunning countryside. He hadn't enjoyed a walk so much in years, he thought to himself afterwards. That evening at home, Steve relaxed with a glass of wine and listened to his favourite music. And now, for the first time in ages, he had company. Pepe sidled up alongside him and lay there quietly until bedtime. "I rather like this," Steve said to himself as he made his way upstairs.

The following day he was due to visit a friend. He telephoned Jane and Sarah and asked them whether it was OK to take Pepe along. He had the injection kit and took some honey along. His friend couldn't believe his eyes when at 4.30 exactly, Steve's mobile phone gave him an alarm call and he injected the dog in the garden. It was the first clue he had got that things were about to change in Steve's life.

The following day, Jane rang from the kennels to check up on things. "We can probably take her back tomorrow," she told Steve.

"Do you have to?" he asked. "Can't she stay with me?"

Quite rightly, Jane didn't think Steve had spent enough time with Pepe for him to be fully aware of the job he was taking on.

"We'll see," she replied. "Keep her for now."

Over the following days, Steve and Pepe's bond grew tighter and tighter. One afternoon, Steve had to go to a meeting. But once more he took Pepe with him. His business contacts looked on bemused as, right on the dot of 4.30, Steve excused himself for a moment. They watched in amazement through the window as Steve climbed into his car to administer the injection to the waiting Pepe.

For the first few weeks, everything went smoothly. Then one morning, Pepe looked distinctly unwell. She was swaying around and looked glazed. Steve had already looked up the symptoms of a diabetic attack in a medical dictionary and guessed Pepe was having one. He rang the kennels immediately and was told to mix honey and water in a particular ratio. Almost immediately after he had given Pepe a spoonful of the mix, she perked up. The panic was over, but it marked a turning point for Steve. That evening he spoke to Jane and Sarah again. "I want to keep her for good," he said.

His friends couldn't fathom why he had decided to take on such a responsibility at that stage of his life. Having seen his children grow up and with his marriage now over, Steve had regained his wings. He was someone who had always loved to travel and enjoyed his sports. Now he was tying himself down to look after a dog that needed more attention than any child or wife ever did. One or two thought he was mad. Yet, to Steve, Pepe had provided him with a new happiness. And it was a relationship that he was determined to work hard at.

Steve and Pepe became inseparable. He took his dog with him everywhere, arming himself with all the medical kit he needed, always willing to put Pepe first. If he was driving along a motorway in the afternoon and he saw a sign for service stations two miles or thirty miles away, he always took the first exit and waited for the clock to reach 4.30. He never risked giving Pepe her shot even a couple of minutes late.

Steve put more and more work into caring for his dog. In the wake of Pepe's one and only attack, Steve hadn't been satisfied with the knowledge he'd gleaned from the medical dictionary, so he began researching Pepe's illness more thoroughly. He went to his local library, devouring every available book on canine illness, and diabetes in particular. He spent hours on the internet, looking up references and reading about other people's experiences with it.

But he didn't stop there. He had a friend who was studying to be a vet. When he mentioned that a lecture on the subject was being held at his college, Steve persuaded him to get him an invitation. Soon he was something of an expert on the subject.

It's a common fallacy that human diabetes is an easily controlled condition, that all you need to do is give the patient a dose of insulin and they'll be all right. In fact, it's a highly variable condition and the levels of

225

insulin needed to stabilise it can change significantly over a short period of time. In humans this means being monitored at all times, and watching out for telltale signs such as glazed eyes and slurred or nonsensical speech. But it is much harder to detect in dogs.

Steve became an expert at detecting changes in Pepe's health. To friends and family she would look perfectly OK, but Steve would know better. He also made sure her condition was monitored medically as often as possible and he became a dab hand at taking urine samples by placing a tin foil tray under Pepe. He also learned how to take blood samples.

In the wrong hands, Pepe would almost certainly not have survived for long. In Steve's hands, she got the best possible chance to survive and thrive. His knowledge of canine diabetes became so great that — at times — it eclipsed that of his local vet.

Unfortunately, Pepe developed other problems, including liver conditions. On one occasion, she was being examined by a young vet at Steve's local practice. The vet was describing the treatment he was going to give Pepe when Steve interrupted him.

"Isn't that going to have an adverse effect on the diabetes?" he asked, politely.

"Oh no, I don't think so," the vet replied, sticking to his guns.

Steve was sure of his ground and suggested a second opinion.

"That's not necessary," the vet said.

"I think it is," said Steve, taking Pepe in his arms and heading for the reception where he made an appointment to meet with the senior vet the following week.

When he visited the following week he found both the senior and junior vets in attendance.

The junior vet explained the problem — and his suggested treatment.

After a quick examination, the older vet looked up and said to his partner: "Yes, quite right."

Steve had held his tongue until now, but couldn't keep quiet any longer. He'd looked up the treatment they'd suggested and knew it would interfere with the insulin Pepe was taking.

"Excuse me, but aren't you forgetting she's got diabetes?" he said to the older vet.

He froze for a moment. "Oh my God, yes," he said.

Within minutes he was writing out a prescription for a totally different treatment, one that was compatible with a diabetic condition.

"We must never imagine we are always right," he told his colleague. "Sometimes the owners can help us."

Five years after she entered Steve's life, Pepe left it. Like so many dogs who rely on large amounts of medication to survive, Pepe developed complications. In the end, Steve had to make the fateful decision to let her go. It was incredibly hard for him. He was devastated by the loss and it took him a long time to recover.

It was in the aftermath of Pepe's death, that I got to know Steve. He and his sister visited me with a view to

227

having one of a litter of English springer spaniels one of my dogs had produced. As I always do, I interviewed the potential owners myself. Steve told me a little of his story. While he spent some time with the dogs, his sister filled me in on what a remarkable owner he had been to his previous dog.

"A friend of mine is in the medical profession and she reckoned Steve was one of the leading experts in the country on diabetes by the end," she said with a look of sisterly pride. I had no hesitation in giving Steve one of my dogs, called Poppet — a name not a million miles removed from his beloved Pepe. We stayed in contact afterwards and became quite friendly.

On one occasion, I remember saying his relationship with his dogs was comparable to a marriage. "If you take a dog on, it's in sickness and in health, for richer for poorer, for better for worse," he said. "It wasn't something that happened in my marriage, but I stayed with Pepe right to the wire."

I knew Pepe had cost him a great deal of money in medical and veterinary bills. One day I asked him whether he had ever regretted taking on the responsibility of Pepe. His response was immediate.

"Oh, of course there were times when I wondered what I'd taken on," he said. "But then she'd just look at me with those big brown eyes of hers and I couldn't imagine life without her."

It was a sentiment that summed up for me something all outstanding owners know at heart. And it is something we can all learn from in one way or another. Yes, Steve had poured his heart and soul into his relationship with Pepe. He had changed his life, done everything in his power to give Pepe a better life. He'd put an awful lot in — but he'd got infinitely more out.

BREATHING SPACE

The benefits of letting
a dog be itself

My paternal grandmother had a great empathy with all animals. She was from Romany stock and had grown up around horses and dogs. She imparted many pieces of wisdom from the comfort of her armchair in the kitchen, but one sticks in my mind more than any other.

I remember my uncle had been trying to get his dog Bruce to do something or other. Whatever it was, Bruce wasn't having any of it. The more Bruce defied him, the more intense my uncle became. Eventually, my grandmother intervened. "Stop fussing over the dog, you'll only make him worse that way," she said. "Give him some time and he'll be all right."

As is so often the case, it took me many years to understand what she meant, let alone fully appreciate its power. Now, however, I see her point clearly. Often it is only by allowing a dog the space to be itself that owners can give them the happiness they deserve. I was reminded of this only recently, in my own back yard, as it were.

★   ★   ★

One dismal, overcast March morning a year or two ago, I looked out of my kitchen window to be greeted by an unfamiliar face. Standing on the grass outside, staring intently back at me, was one of the most pathetic-looking creatures I had ever encountered.

The dog was probably between fifteen and eighteen months old, and was a cross between a German shepherd and something else. He was black and tan, but his coat was a sticky, muddy mess and he looked as if he had been dragged through a hedge backwards; the poor creature was so wet and cold that he was shivering non-stop. Such was his rundown state, that his ears were at right angles to each other, the right one flopping over his right eye, the left one turned out to the side. It was as if he was using them to send a signal by semaphore. If he was trying to get a message across, it was soon obvious what it was. As I walked outside and moved closer, I could see the dog was absolutely terrified. He was also starving.

It looked as if he hadn't eaten for a long while. His ribs were showing and you could almost have got your fingers around his waist he was so painfully thin. Every now and again he let out a little whine, as if to plead for any spare scraps of food we might have. But there was something else in his face, a plaintive, pleading sort of gaze in his eye. It was as if he was asking me, "Am I safe here?"

A day or so earlier, I'd heard in the village about a supposedly abandoned dog that had been seen wandering in nearby Laughton Woods.

231

I occasionally take my dogs for a walk there, so I had headed off in the hope of finding the stray and taking him to a rescue centre. I'd had no luck. Now I wondered whether this was the same dog. It clearly looked as if it had been living rough for a time. But if it was, what had brought it to my front door?

I wasn't alone that morning. My partner Glenn was inside and Charlotte, the young girl who was helping me with the dogs and my horses, had been in the stables and had also seen the dog. As I emerged from the house, she was making a slow, steady move in his direction. Charlotte has a natural affinity for animals; inching her way towards the dog, her body language was gentle and soothing. As she tried to coax the dog towards her, she made herself as warm and welcoming as she could. But the instant she got within a few feet of him, he shot off down the lane leading to the village.

I told Charlotte not to worry. I had an inkling that he might return and, sure enough, a few minutes later, he reappeared, picking his way carefully back to the spot where he'd been standing. Charlotte and I knew the important thing now was to gain the dog's trust, so we sat down by the stables and waited. Over the next twenty minutes, the same routine repeated itself. The dog would inch closer to us, then at the first sign of movement or even a sound from us it would suddenly run off again.

During one of the dog's disappearing acts, Glenn had appeared with a bowl of meat and biscuits. He'd seen what had been going on from a distance and sensed what was needed to draw the dog into the yard.

It worked a treat. The sight of the bowl sitting there near the gate leading to the yard proved impossible to resist. Slowly the dog began shuffling his way towards us. We just sat there quietly, silently trying to will him towards the bowl. It still took another ten minutes for him to start eating. The air of relief that passed through the three of us when he finally found the courage to dive into the bowl was tangible.

As I watched him eating away, my thoughts now turned to the practicalities of reporting him to the authorities. I knew this was the next, proper step, although I couldn't help feeling reluctant to do it. Fortunately, Annette the local dog warden is a friend. Her van pulled up in the drive within half an hour or so.

She went through the legalities of the situation, asking me what I knew about him, how he'd come to be here, what was his name, breed and so on. "The answer to all those questions is the same, Annette. I haven't got a clue," I told her. The dog had no tag or form of identification on him. He was a mystery.

Annette's job now was to take the dog to an approved sanctuary, then go through the correct procedures. While we went through the formalities together, the dog had sat quietly by. His meal had calmed his mood a lot. He seemed less frightened, although there was still a real sense of nervousness about him.

With all her paperwork done, Annette made a move towards him.

"Let's get him in the van," she said.

As she led him away, the dog looked over his shoulder at me and Charlotte. It was as if to say: "What have I done wrong? I thought I was safe here. I thought you liked me?"

Charlotte was a bit tearful about this. She understood what had to be done, but that didn't make it any easier to see such a vulnerable creature taken off into such an uncertain future. Annette told me she'd keep him for a week in a registered rescue centre. After that he'd be put up for adoption.

I knew the procedure pretty well, but couldn't stop myself asking, "You're not going to put him down, are you?"

"No, Jan, don't worry," she replied.

As she closed the door I could see the dog's piercing eyes looking out at me. I felt emotional but consoled myself with the knowledge that at least he was safe now and no further harm was going to come to him.

Annette drove away with the dog in the van. Back in the house, we all looked at each other, unable to speak. The silence went on for a good minute before Charlotte broke it by saying, "When can we go and get him?"

We had left a message at the rescue centre before Annette had arrived back there.

The week went by and no one came to claim the dog, so Charlotte and I drove back to the rescue centre and collected him. As we arrived at the small kennel and run that had been his home for the past seven days, he was waiting there, alert. The staff at the rescue centre had fed and wormed him and he had put on a little weight during his time there. I could see he was on the road to recovery. At the sound of my voice he wagged his tail.

"How you doing, fella?" I asked.

As Annette opened the gate to the kennel he charged at me and Charlotte. He didn't know where he wanted to go, but he wanted to go somewhere. He was saying: "Let's get out of here."

He sat in our van as good as gold. At home we couldn't introduce him to the rest of the dogs straight away. We therefore gave him a nice kennel and run on his own, near the office where he could see us coming and going.

No one was more devoted to our new arrival than Charlotte. Her heart had really gone out to him when he'd turned up and she was overjoyed when we brought him home again. As the new boy settled in, Charlotte became his closest human friend. It was while she was out walking him at the back of the house that I saw how tight the bond was becoming.

We hadn't been able to think of a name for the dog. I judge whether a name is right or not by a dog's reaction to it. If the dog responds then it works — if not, then it's back to the drawing board. We had tried a variety of names — Prince, Paris, Toby — but none of them had worked.

Glenn and I were out near Charlotte one morning when we heard her calling him to her. "Come on, Rocky," she said, instinctively.

The dog turned and looked at her instantly.

"That'll do," Glenn and I said in unison.

The first few weeks were difficult. Rocky was a very suspicious dog and could be edgy at times. The way he weighed up everyone who came near him reminded me of another of my grandmother's sayings: "Beware instant friends." If anything, Charlotte and I were even more apprehensive. Even though we were now Rocky's legal owners, we still wondered whether his real owner would turn up.

When a friend called me one day to say she'd seen two posters asking for the return of stray dogs in the past week, we couldn't stop ourselves heading off to look at both them. One was in Scunthorpe, the other in Barnetby. On both occasions we went through the same emotions. As we hurriedly scanned the pictures of the two dogs — a black terrier cross, and a tan and white Labrador — we felt sorry for the owners who'd lost them. But we both confessed to feeling huge relief as well.

The rumours of a dog living rough in the woods stopped immediately we took Rocky in. Either there hadn't been a dog at all — or else we had him safely at home with us. As we got to know him better, there was no doubt it was the latter. At the first sight of a cat, a rabbit or a bird, Rocky would go ballistic, chasing after them if he could. It was obvious that he had grown used to fending for himself and saw them as potential food.

It was also obvious that, somewhere in his past, Rocky had been abused. There were no discernible marks where he had been hit, but from the way he reacted around strangers there was no question he had been subjected to violence. If someone raised their arm suddenly near him, he would duck. And if anybody raised their voices or moved quickly to reach for something, he became very agitated.

One day a friend arrived. He didn't know I had taken in Rocky and was immediately moved by his story. Rocky was lying down not far from me. The friend suddenly jumped up and went over to give him a consoling cuddle. Rocky got so upset he wet himself.

He was most relaxed when he was with Charlotte. Even then, she had to be very careful out walking him when there were other people around. It had been a long time since I'd had a rescue dog and I had forgotten the joy to be derived from giving a stable, loving home to a mistreated dog. And I had also forgotten the hard work that goes into rehabilitating them.

The first rescue dog I ever took in was Barmie, a Jack Russell with real character that I came across at a local rescue centre. Like Rocky, he'd been in a terrible state — he was found on waste land attached to a rope that had been tied to a concrete block. Unlike Rocky, he bore the bruises and scars of his abuse.

A lot of people, even the rescue centre owner who knew me well, thought I'd taken on too much in Barmie. And there were times during the difficult early days when I agreed with them. Barmie's road to recovery was a long one. It took me many months of hard work to win his trust. He would stand under the kitchen table growling at me, and generally removed himself from the rest of the world. His past associations were so bad, you couldn't blame him; it was a purely defensive instinct. Slowly, though, I had restored his faith in humans and the wider world.

Rocky's journey was going to be even longer, mainly because he was an independent spirit. Whereas Barmie was a smaller, physically weak dog, Rocky was a tough customer. He'd learned to live on his own, he was a survivor. In truth, he didn't actually need us.

Charlotte sensed this and gave him the breathing space he needed. Dogs are independent creatures, capable of surviving on their own, and Charlotte understood this. Even when he was behaving well, she knew there was a certain distance between Rocky and the rest of the world. We tried putting him in with other dogs, less threatening members of the family, mainly from "the girls" within the pack. But he never bonded with any of them — in fact, he didn't seem to want to know.

On top of this, Rocky would run off occasionally. There were days when Charlotte and I wondered whether that was the last we'd ever see of him. In truth, there were times when we wondered whether he would be happier roaming free like that. Now and again Charlotte would ask out loud whether we were actually doing him any favours in keeping him. "He's a happy hobo," she used to say, "he's quite content with his own company."

The more we got to know him, the more obvious it was why he'd come to our home rather than any other in the area. Clearly, he had formed a bad association with built-up areas and roads. He didn't like being around them. My guess was that he had settled on us as a potential home because it was so isolated. We were at the end of a quiet lane. Beyond us there were only open fields. If he needed to run for the open spaces he could do so.

It took a long time for Rocky to find some kind of peace again. When that moment arrived, however, it was well worth the wait. One day Charlotte was out in the field with him, trying to encourage him to play — something he still didn't do with any natural enthusiasm. Suddenly, he turned and charged up to her, running exuberantly through the long grass. It was something he'd never done before. I could see the joy in his heart and it was a privilege to watch.

Patience wasn't the only quality Charlotte demonstrated that year. As summer turned to autumn, she began spending more and more time with Rocky. One weekend she was going home to visit her parents. She asked whether she could take Rocky with her. I was a little apprehensive, but trusted her.

"If you think it's going to be all right," I said.

"Don't worry, I'll make sure Mum and Dad treat him the right way," she reassured me.

When she came back the following Monday, I wasn't at all surprised to discover Rocky had had a great time. He'd settled into the home easily and had spent most of the weekend curled up in front of the fire. Her parents weren't the greatest dog lovers in the world, but they'd been more than happy to have him in the home. "He's such a good boy," her mother had said.

It was when he returned to his run at our home that we first noticed the change in him. His area there was spacious and heated. But that night we heard him crying. It wasn't so much a howl as a painful whining. When Charlotte heard it, the tears welled up in her eyes immediately. The pattern repeated itself the next time Charlotte took him home to her parents. Once more he relaxed as soon as he got there and was much more receptive to her requests.

We'd had him with us for six months by now. It had been a long, slow process, but — mainly thanks to Charlotte — Rocky had been transformed. And so had Charlotte. Charlotte loved him to bits, that was clear for anyone to see. The job of caring for Rocky had really brought out the best in her. Just how much she had matured became clear when she returned once more from a weekend away. Again, Rocky had become a little more tense and noticeably more distant when he'd got back to us and the other dogs.

"He's happy here, but he could be even happier, couldn't he?" Charlotte asked me out of the blue.

I hesitated for a moment, guessing what she meant. I knew she was the kind of person who would put a dog's welfare ahead of her own, but wasn't quite sure that she wanted me to confirm what was becoming obvious.

"Yes, he could," I said, tentatively.

Charlotte and I both knew that what Rocky needed now was a home that suited him better, somewhere where he could be the only dog within a loving family.

"I'd thought about it, but hadn't said anything in case it upset you," I said.

240

"It's not about me, it's about Rocky," Charlotte replied.

It was just after her seventeenth birthday, but she had quickly acquired a wisdom way beyond her years. Many owners would never have had the courage or selflessness to face up to things the way she was now doing. At that moment, she repaid all the faith I'd put in her when first giving her a job.

We knew finding a proper home for Rocky wasn't going to be easy. We had to find exactly the right family and exactly the right setup for him. I'm a great believer in fate and just got on with things, quietly confident that the answer would present itself in due course. And it did.

Soon afterwards I was running one of my courses. Among the students that week was a lady called Vanessa, whose dog Scud I had helped in the past. We had become close and she'd taken one of my springer puppies, Haggis. During a break in the classes, we were chatting away. She saw Charlotte out in the fields walking with Rocky.

"That's your stray, is it?" she asked.

"Yes, that's Rocky," I replied, before explaining the situation. "He deserves a bit better than we can give him I think, Vanessa."

A couple of days later, Vanessa was on the phone.

She was friendly with a couple who had lost their German shepherd a year earlier. They'd taken their time before having another dog, but were now ready to look and were inclined to take a rescue dog.

241

"Would you mind if I mentioned Rocky to them?" Vanessa asked me.

I trusted Vanessa's instincts. She knew the kind of owners we were looking for.

It couldn't have been much more than fifteen minutes later that the phone rang again and a woman called Karen was on the line.

She introduced herself as Vanessa's friend. We got talking and — encouraged by what I heard — I invited her over to meet Rocky.

Karen and her husband Nick lived in Oxford. They made the long drive up to Lincolnshire a couple of days later. Given Rocky's nature, we didn't rush things. I explained to them that he was something of a loner. They said they understood. When we went out into the fields with him, Rocky didn't really want to know Nick and Karen. I put him on a lead and when Karen took it, he gave her a withering look, as if to say: "Who the hell are you?"

It was, of course, Rocky being Rocky; Rocky being wary of instant friends. But it did worry me a little. Nick and Karen stayed for a couple of hours, chatting. They talked a little about their old dog. I was glad to hear that they weren't looking for an exact replica of him. They said that Rocky was very different, something that reassured me.

When they left, they said they'd call in the next day or so. To be honest, I wouldn't have blamed them for rejecting Rocky. Most people want a dog that gives something back to them, and look for what it is going to bring to their lives — not the other way around.

That evening, however, Karen was on the phone.

"Jan, Nick and I have talked it through and we feel the same way. If ever a dog deserved to have a lot of time and effort put into him, then it's Rocky. If you're willing for us to have him, we'd love to give him a home," she said.

I said "yes" immediately. It was clear to me that here were two people who were going to do whatever it took to make Rocky happy. They weren't getting him just for their own pleasure — though doubtless he would bring them lots of it. You don't often hear people talk like that.

There were a lot of tears when they came to collect him. Charlotte was there to pass on all the bits and pieces of knowledge she'd accumulated during the eventful six months since Rocky had arrived at our door. Like me, she sensed we were entrusting him to the very best owners imaginable.

"We'd like to think that in six months time he'll be looking at us the way he looks at you two," Karen said to me and Charlotte.

Rocky was one of the strongest and most powerful personalities I have come across in recent years. He really lit up our lives for the brief period he was with us, and he exemplifies the way that some dogs have an ability to bring out the best in people. He'd done it with Charlotte, and I could see he was going to do it again with Karen and Nick. But more importantly, he reminded me of two things that are fundamental.

As humans, we are far too hung up on the past. We spend interminable amounts of time dwelling on what happened earlier in our lives and how this has affected us. Dog owners are often guilty of doing the same, particularly when they have rescue dogs. It is natural that we should want to know what happened to them, what dreadful thing drove them to the rescue centre in the first place. And in nursing a rescue dog back to good health, it's helpful to know as much as you can about what happened to them. But as far as psychology is concerned, we are never, ever going to know what our dogs are thinking. We can't even know whether they have any lasting memory of the past that would influence the way they live in the future in any deep and meaningful way. Rocky reminded me that dogs seem to want to get on with their lives. While they learn from the experience of the past, in general they seem more focused on the future. We should follow their lead.

The second thing he reminded me of was to do with respect. As I've said already, respect is a quality that is absolutely central to our relationship with our dogs. I strongly believe that respect should extend to an understanding of our dogs' individual personalities and characters. One of the things I am most proud of when it comes to my method of "dog listening", is the way it allows dogs to be themselves. Dogs that respond well to the method find themselves freed from the yoke of leadership and learn to relax and express themselves again. It is akin to seeing a human weighed down with responsibility suddenly having that burden lifted off their shoulders. You can literally see the relief in their faces.

Of course, the personalities that are liberated vary wildly. What Rocky showed me was that some dogs are natural loners, with a strong need for space and freedom. By giving him that space, Charlotte had restored his faith in humans. It was a valuable lesson, and one I won't forget in a hurry.

A DOG'S BEST FRIEND

Why great owners just want to give their dogs the best

Dog owners are generally compassionate and caring people — sometimes excessively so. Too many people I meet make the mistake of what I call "guilt shifting" — taking the blame for situations that are beyond their control. I have frequently heard owners complain that they wished they could take in all the rescue dogs in the world and make them right. Obviously, this is impossibly unrealistic, like trying to save the planet single-handedly.

But this isn't to say that we should do nothing. Just as we can do our bit to help the environment by recycling, driving in lead-free fuelled cars and leaving the car at home when it's at all possible, I believe we can all make a difference as dog owners too. If we live with our dogs the right way — that is to say, in a way that is respectful, compassionate and based on an understanding of the dog's true nature — and if we educate as many people to share our philosophy, we might just be able to make this a better world for all its canines.

246

Having said all that, every once in a while I do come across someone who makes me wonder whether they might really be able to save the world's dogs single-handedly. Such a person was Brian.

Brian ran a second-hand car showroom and garage in Leeds. The business was his life — he had poured body and soul into it and had been well rewarded.

Brian's success owed much to his attitude. Unlike so many secondhand car dealers, he never gave the impression he was trying to rip his customers off or con them. Many of his customers were buying their very first cars. He believed in giving them the best car they could possibly afford. His motto was "everyone deserves the best they can get". People respected that — and he prospered as a result.

Brian was single so he spent almost all his time at work. He had never seriously considered having dogs; he'd liked them as a boy, but his work meant that in purely practical terms he didn't have time for them. All that changed one day when he met a friend who had just returned from a visit to the city's council-run rescue centre.

The friend had discovered a stray dog wandering the streets that morning. There was something about the dog that had made her feel sorry for it. It was a smallish, black crossbreed, a very affectionate-looking dog. It looked lost and unhappy, and badly in need of some tender loving care. She had been unsure what to do at first, but after a couple of phone calls was told she should take it to the rescue centre, where she would go through the formalities of filing an official report.

This she did and she left there without considering what was going to happen to the dog next. As the day had worn on, however, this had begun to play on her mind more and more. She asked Brian whether he knew. He didn't, so he suggested she call the rescue centre back.

The centre is run according to guidelines that are handed down by the RSPCA to establishments of this kind. Basically, if a dog isn't claimed within seven days it is put down. I am not going to pretend this is something I agree with — I don't, particularly given that these centres are supposedly dedicated to the "protection" of animals.

When Brian's friend learnt this and told him, he was pretty incredulous too. "I can't believe that's right," he said. This played on Brian's mind over the next few days. He kept wondering whether the stray's owners had turned up to collect him. Eventually, he couldn't handle the uncertainty any more and he went down to the sanctuary with his friend.

To their disappointment, the dog was still there. No one had turned up to claim him. Once more the staff confirmed the fate that now awaited the stray. "He's been here six days so far, so if someone doesn't come by the end of tomorrow, I'm afraid we'll have to put him down," he was told. Brian's friend was in tears. He took her for a coffee around the corner while they tried to think what to do.

"We've got to do something," he said. Half an hour later he was back inside the sanctuary.

"I'll take her," he said. He paid the £20 necessary and drove off.

But, Brian hadn't given it any thought whatsoever. He arrived back at his garage with the dog and realised he didn't even have a place for the dog to sleep. He called in a couple of lads from the workshop and got them to clear out some storage space at the back of the office building. He then popped out and got a few bits and pieces from his nearest pet shop. Brian often spent the night in the garage, so he stayed there with the dog that night too.

Over the following days and weeks, Brian bonded with his new friend. But the closer he got to him, the more he began to think about all the other stray dogs that wouldn't be rescued in this way.

It didn't make sense to him that perfectly healthy, loving dogs like this one were being killed for no reason other than there was nowhere to put them. He resolved to stay in contact with the rescue centre and intervene if there were any more dogs on "death row", as he called it.

It wasn't long before he was called into action. A few weeks later the phone went. It was the rescue centre. Six days earlier they'd taken in a bitch that was in whelp. No one had been in to claim her, so now the dog — and her unborn puppies — were twenty-four hours away from being given a lethal injection. To Brian this was even more of an outrage. He took the dog back with him and cleared a little more space in his stores.

A few weeks later he was the proud owner of ten dogs. The bitch had produced a litter of eight lovely puppies. Brian knew he couldn't look after all these dogs, so he enlisted the help of the local radio station. They ran a story about Brian's work — and the puppies who now needed a home. It wasn't long before Brian had found eight good, respectable families willing to give them a fair start in life.

No sooner had he done this, than he had received another phone call from the rescue centre — and then another. Soon he was taking in a dog every few weeks. Suddenly he felt like a man on a mission.

Brian was a highly responsible man. He knew he was getting into something serious, so he spoke to the local council and began the process of applying for a licence as a recognised animal sanctuary. Of course, he got more than his fair share of funny looks and disbelieving comments. "But your premises are a garage and a car showroom," people would say. But when people came down to see the building they were flabbergasted. Since making the decision to become a sanctuary, Brian had completely rearranged his premises. He had cleared a large storeroom at the back of the office building which he could use to house the dogs, and he hired carpenters to convert them into kennels and individual quarters for the animals. Planning officials turned up ready to see the worst, then left quietly shaking their heads when they found probably the best equipped sanctuary for miles around.

Bureaucrats being bureaucrats, the application took its time. The licence process got held up here and there, but each time it did Brian patiently dealt with the appropriate official, smoothing out any problems and easing the application to the final acceptance stage.

With the licence finally granted, the rescue centre soon began taking in a dog almost every week and Brian's determination to give his dogs the best deepened. He ploughed much of the profits from his car showroom into equipping the centre with medical facilities, play facilities, feeding areas and play areas — everything a dog needed to make its life comfortable. He also enlisted the services of a group of volunteers.

Brian's work was exemplary in every way possible. He had a one hundred per cent record in rehousing the dogs he rescued — and at the same time he worked hard to make sure each animal went to the right home. He didn't want to see them back at the rescue centre six months later. He vetted owners carefully and — uniquely in my experience — worked with them to make sure the dogs settled into their new homes.

Brian's qualities are too numerous to list here. He has all those attributes I have outlined in this book — and plenty more to spare. Above all, I think he displayed a determination to do the right thing and an ability to put up with bureaucracy and small-mindedness that would put a saint to shame. This latter quality was never better illustrated than in an incident which could have had terrible consequences for his rescue centre.

I don't know why this should be, but success inevitably brings negative responses as well. There were those who resented or objected to Brian's work for some reason, and it was probably one of these people who called in the RSPCA.

"I'm afraid I have received a serious complaint about your treatment of the dogs," announced the inspector who turned up at the garage unannounced one morning.

Brian was lost for words for a moment. He knew he had nothing to hide, yet at the same time he imagined the repercussions if the inspector saw something he didn't like. It might mean the end of the sanctuary.

"What do you mean?" he eventually asked.

The inspector told him that he'd been reported by a member of the public who'd seen him in a local park "cramming a dozen dogs into the back of a small van".

Brian asked the inspector if he'd like to see his van. Brian had recently spent a small fortune on a brand-new Mercedes van. It was a distinctive yellow and had been customised specifically to carry dogs. The inspector's face registered surprise when he saw it. "Are you sure this is the only van you've got?" he said.

"Yes," said Brian. "And this is what I had out this morning."

The look of bafflement on the inspector's face deepened when Brian slid open one of the side doors. The interior of the van was immaculate. Inside he saw a series of specially built cages. There were four smaller cages, suitable for holding a smaller breed, like a terrier, two medium sized cages capable of holding at least two bigger dogs and two very large cages, capable of holding three or four average size dogs. As if this was not convincing enough, there was food, a couple of first aid kits and blankets. Brian's van put the RSPCA man's own vehicle to shame.

"How many dogs did you have out this morning?" the inspector asked.

"I had all my dogs out, all six of them," Brian replied.

The inspector scribbled something down and shook his head. But he hadn't finished yet.

"Could I see the dogs?" he asked. "The report claims one of them was limping very badly and needs medical attention."

Brian smiled quietly to himself.

"Ah, that'll be Sherry, she does limp a bit," he said.

The inspector perked up a bit at this. "Could I see her, please?" he said.

"Of course," replied Brian.

Sherry had arrived at Brian's sanctuary a year or so earlier in a terrible state, she was run-down, emaciated and generally neglected. But her biggest problem had been one of her legs, which was so badly damaged that she couldn't stand on it. When Brian had taken her to the vet, he'd told Brian there was no option but to amputate the limb. Brian had footed the bill, along with the cost of keeping her in hospital for the first week or so of her recovery.

Sherry was a brave little dog and had dealt with her disability admirably. Somehow, Brian had never been able to part with her, so she had become the first of his dogs to become a permanent resident of the rescue centre. Sherry was a happy little dog and, as she emerged from the kennel area, she hopped towards the

RSPCA inspector looking as if she didn't have a care in the world.

The inspector's face couldn't have presented a starker contrast. He took one look at Sherry picking her way across the yard on her three legs, before putting away his pen and shutting the file he was carrying.

"It would appear someone has been wasting my time and yours," he said, with an apologetic shake of his head. "I'll be on my way."

I first met Brian not long after this had happened. I'll never forget that first encounter with him — I had heard of his sanctuary and his work with animals but hadn't been told about his alternative career. So when I first walked into the garage and saw the cars and motorbikes in the repair shop, I'd thought I'd gone mad.

It was only inside his office that I got the first hint that I might after all be in the right place. There were two dogs lying next to Brian's desk.

Stepping into the rear of the building was like stepping into another world. The noise and activity of the workshop gave way to the perfect peace of a haven for dogs. There must have been a dozen or so dogs in various pens and kennels, each of them as calm and contented as could be. To these dogs, this must have seemed like a small slice of heaven here on Earth. It seemed pretty close to me, as well.

I have chosen to end this book with Brian's story for a number of reasons. In a world where few people are willing to look beyond themselves, he is an example of someone who has reshaped his life in order to provide a sanctuary for animals that have been given up for dead by the rest of society. On a daily basis, he shows a blend of courage and compassion, selflessness and determination that should be an example to every dog owner. But I have also left him to last for another, simpler reason.

Brian's philosophy is the same whether he is dealing with his human or canine customers. Whether selling a saloon or saving the life of a stray, his belief is that we all deserve the best. It's a sentiment that I, for one, wholeheartedly support. Here's to a world in which everyone lives by the example of great dog owners like Brian.

ACKNOWLEDGEMENTS

This, my fourth book, has been a pleasure to write for one particular reason. Too often these days we are exposed to the negative side of our relationship with our animals, specifically the cruelty some people display towards the creatures who share our world. In writing this book, it has been such a joy to be able to illustrate the other side of the coin, to focus on the positive, selfless work so many owners put in to improve their dog's lives. More than anything, I'd like to thank those wonderful individuals who provided me with the inspiration to do this.

Once again the process of shaping my thoughts into book form has been assisted by a special group of people.

Firstly the team at HarperCollins, especially Monica Chakraverty, and secondly at Gillon Aitken, where I have been helped once more by my agent Mary Pachnos and her colleagues. Mary over the years has guided me as both my trusted agent and good friend. Her skills in the world of publishing have been marvellous, but it is for her commitment to my work that I value her the most.

At home, I owe a huge debt of gratitude to my team. My son Tony Knight combines his work helping owners as a Dog Listener with instructing the students who attend our canine communications course. I admire and love him for his dedication and professionalism. Then there is Charlotte Medley — our Charlie — who cares for and loves our pets as we do. Whatever she is doing, she is always prepared to go that extra yard and is a joy to be with.

Last but not least is Glenn Miller, my partner and the person who provides the vital "backroom" support that every successful team needs, whether it's organising flights or preparing our dogs for the few shows that we have time to attend. His love and support is very special, and I'd like to thank him for it.

Jan Fennell